THE POWER OF JUST DOING STUFF

"It's like whoah, when we get together, it's like everyone is feeding everyone else. There's this atmosphere of 'I tell you . . . you tell me'. Everyone listens, then someone comes up with another idea. It's like collective excitement, collective inspiration, collective knowledge, coming together for the profit of the group. You can feel the thrill."
Emiliano Muñoz, Portillo en Transición

"Once practical things start happening that people can see and touch, something changes in the culture. It feels like something is happening, that the reality is changing."
José Martín, Coín en Transición

"Energy, solar panels or whatever, are just a way to get there. We're not wedded to solar panels, or combined heat and power, or whatever. We're wedded to well-being."
Agamemnon Otero, Brixton Energy

THE POWER
OF JUST
DOING STUFF

How local action can change the world

ROB HOPKINS

Founder of the
Transition movement

First published in 2013 by
UIT / Green Books
PO Box 145, Cambridge CB4 1GQ, UK
www.greenbooks.co.uk
+44 1223 302 041

Design by Jayne Jones

Unless otherwise indicated, all photographs are by the author.

ISBN: 978 0 85784 117 9 (paperback)
ISBN: 978 0 85784 119 3 (ePub)
ISBN: 978 0 85784 129 2 (Kindle)
ISBN: 978 0 85784 118 6 (pdf)

Printed by CPI Group (UK) Ltd, Croydon, CR0 4YY

Disclaimer: The advice herein is believed to be correct at the time
of printing, but the author and publishers accept no liability for
actions inspired by this book.

The author and publishers have endeavoured to contact all
copyright holders, but will be glad to correct in future
editions any inadvertent omissions drawn to their notice.

10 9 8 7 6 5 4 3 2 1

Contents

Acknowledgements

I'd like to thank the team at Transition Network: Kat Balassa, Sophy Banks, Ben Brangwyn, Isabel Carlisle, Jo Coish, Naresh Giangrande, Nicola Hillary, Peter Lipman, Sarah McAdam, Ed Mitchell, Filipa Pimentel, Amber Ponton, Fiona Ward, Laura Whitehead, as well as Lou Brown, Charlotte Du Cann, Hal Gillmore, Mike Grenville, Tony Graham, Jacqi Hodgson, Shane Hughes, Frances Northrop, Mary Popham and Jay Tompt.

Also the people who gave their time so generously while I was researching this book: Kevin Anderson, Peter Andrews, Christopher Bear, Ruth Ben-Tovim, Rachel Bodle, Cristiano Bottone, Peter Capener, Robert Cervelli, Tina Clarke, Helen Cunningham, Rachel de Thample, Juan del Rio, Peter Driscoll, Edward Droste, Joe Duggan, Alex Edleson, Hide Enomoto, Simon Gershon, Don Hall, Brian Harper, Colin Harrison, Jo Homan, Pierre Houben, Andrew Knox, Duncan Law, José Martín, Catriona Mulligan, Ciaran Mundy, Emiliano Muñoz, Lucy Neal, Anna O'Brien, Agamemnon Otero, Jules Peck, Monica Picavea, Filipa Pimentel, Joanne Poyourow, Philip Revell, Daniel Rossen, Chris Rowland, Martin Shaw, Nicholas Shaxson, Andrew Simms, Steve Smith, Sarah Stewart, Sónia Tavares, Chris Taylor, Graham Truscott, Simon Turner, Peter Victor and Jon Walker, as well as the readers of TransitionCulture.org for their input, and everyone whose photos are used here.

Tudor Trust, Roger Ross of Lots Road Auction, Theresa Field, Esmée Fairbairn Foundation, V. Kann Rasmussen Foundation, John Ellerman Foundation, the Roddick Foundation, Calouste Gulbenkian Foundation, Polden-Puckham Charitable Foundation,

The Bromley Trust, The Network for Social Change, Nominet Trust, Ashoka, Artists Project Earth, the Marmot Charitable Trust, The European Economic and Social Committee Civil Society Prize, The Arts and Humanities Research Council, Grundtvig Programme, LUSH, the Keep the Land Foundation, Carnegie UK Trust, Curry Stone Design Prize, Transition Tyndale, the Tanner Trust, the Prairie Trust, an anonymous Foundation and many individuals to whom we are very grateful for their support of the evolution of Transition.

Everyone who sent in comments, photos, drawings and so on, and as always, the good people at Green Books.

Dedications:

To the memory of Transition pioneer
Adrienne Campbell.

To the locksmiths of Pamplona.

For Emma, Rowan, Finn, Arlo and Cian.

Might this market in Santander, Spain (above, see page 31), the community in London planting hops in back gardens (below left, see page 73) and the city of Bristol printing its own money (below right, see page 56) represent the seeds of a much-needed new approach to our economic future? *Credits: Guy Milnes (below left); Mark Simmons (below right)*

Introduction

This book is an invitation to explore a new approach to how our economy might work, how we create employment and wealth, and how we live and work in our local communities. Around the world, people are coming together and making this happen. From Argentina to Italy and from Canada to Japan, you will hear through what it looks like and feels like when people decide that they want a different kind of future from the one currently on offer.

You will hear of people's successes and failures, of the moments when the hairs on the back of their necks stand up; when the future feels thrilling. You will hear of what it feels like when you step across from thinking about probabilities to focusing instead on possibilities. In our search for new sources of energy to mobilise our economies, the great surge of creative energy that this approach can unleash may turn out to be the most important one of all.

This book won't tell you what to do (although you'll find some great resources at the back). Rather, it will present you with a new Big Idea for where we move forward to from here, and will give you a taste of what moving towards that looks and feels like. You will hear from creative and imaginative souls who have already set out into uncharted waters. You'll find that these people are not all that different from you. In these pages I want to give you a sense of what preparing for such a journey is like.

I hope that this proves sufficiently inspiring that in later years you might look back at the moment when you picked up this book as having been one of the seminal moments in your life, beyond which you never looked at things in the same way again.

CHAPTER ONE

WHY WE NEED TO DO SOMETHING

How good a society does human nature permit? How good a human nature does society permit?

Abraham Maslow, psychologist (1971)[1]

Why we need a new Big Idea

I have a lot of sympathy for governments that see the imme-
diate problems and strive to deal with them, but I have much
less sympathy if they don't have a longer-term vision that
makes sense of where we're heading. I'm very concerned
that trying to pull out all the stops to re-stimulate economies,
to use the cliché 'to get back on track', is actually a formula
for far worse things to happen, probably in the not-too-
distant future.
Peter Victor, author, *Managing without Growth*[2]

The idea underpinning this book is that local action can change
the world. Between the things we can do as individuals and the
things that governments and business can do to respond to the
challenges of our times, lies a great untapped potential, what I am
calling 'The Power of Just Doing Stuff'. It's about what you can
create with the help of the people who live in your street, your
neighbourhood, your town. I want to excite you about the possibilities of what we can create in the communities around us, and
how, if enough of us do it, it can lead to real impact, to real jobs,
and to real transformation of the places we live and beyond.

One of the reasons I wrote this book was that in late 2012 I
attended a two-day meeting of local authority Chief Executive
Officers from across a region of the UK: an annual occasion for
them to relax with each other, share new ideas and be exposed to
some new thinking. I was there as part of the 'new thinking' bit,
but the most fascinating part was at the beginning, where each
was asked to share where they thought we are headed economically. Are we headed for a gradual return to growth, a bumping
along a plateau for a while, or a more sustained contraction? I
expected most to speak enthusiastically of the new era of growth

lying just around the corner, given that that would be what they are stating publically.

In the event, only about a quarter of them shared that kind of optimism. One said "If we ever get out of this recession, nothing will be as it was in the past." Another said "Every generation has had things better than its parents. Not any more." And another, "Future generations will look back and say this was the start of the end of the Western world." The one that stunned me the most was the man who said that he was fascinated by history, and had been reading about the last days of the Roman Empire in England, where in AD 308 there were roads, agriculture, central heating and so on, and 20 years later the country was back in the Iron Age. "No civilisation has lasted forever," he said. "There is a very real chance of collapse."

It was compelling to hear, in that safe space where people felt comfortable with each other, these honest assessments and deep concerns about our situation. In public, of course, these CEOs would be talking up the 'growth agenda', but here they were stating that they just didn't believe it. I have seen the same thing on several occasions since, when I have spoken to people in similar positions who have confided that they have little or no faith that we will ever see economic growth such as we have known in recent decades again. In this book we will go on to look at the reasons why I think that a relentless growth in GDP is no longer an appropriate or desirable idea, and why I think these public leaders were right to be concerned. Their comments reminded me of the story of The Emperor's New Clothes, and how it took a child to point out what everyone knew – that the Emperor was naked.

Current thinking across Europe seems to be that in order to re-stimulate growth we have to remove all obstacles to business doing what it wants to do wherever it wants to do it, and we need big infrastructure projects. The thinking seems to be that if only businessmen can travel faster on high-speed trains, that somehow the economy will haul itself up off the stretcher and start growing again. That if we build new airports, more businessmen will fly into them and create new businesses that will fuel the economy. That growth, in and of itself, is always a Good Thing.

The irony, of course, is that in a world of increasingly scarce resources, with a climate nearing its tipping point into runaway climate change, and an economy groaning beneath staggering levels of debt, this kind of approach is the last thing we need; this is the last kind of economic activity we need.

'Austerity' versus the 'New Deal'

At the moment, when the future of our economy and the question of how we might get out of our financial hole are debated, we hear only two contrasting stories as to where next. I propose that it's time for a third story to take its place by their side – in debates on TV, on the radio, online, at parties . . .

The first story we'll call 'Austerity': the idea that we need to cut back government spending in the same way that you might prune a rose bush back hard in the hope of stimulating fresh growth. In practice this means deep cuts in public services, economic hardship and a widening gap between rich and poor, all with the promise that this will lead to renewed economic growth at some point. The second option, which we'll call the 'New Deal', suggests that actually what we need to do is to borrow more money from future generations to spend on trying to stimulate renewed economic activity. Some propose a 'Green New Deal', where money is borrowed in order to stimulate the shift to a low-carbon – but still growth-based – economy.

> "The austerity versus Keynsian spending debate is about as useful as arguing whether the Earth is flat or sitting on the back of a pile of turtles."
> Graham Barnes, The Foundation for the Economics of Sustainability (FEASTA) (2013)[3]

The Austerity story recognises that we have partied too hard, that rather than just coming up with more clever mechanisms for dumping our huge accumulated debts on to future generations we need to be grown-up about the debt crisis and get our excesses under control, to learn to cut our coats to suit our cloth. It is interesting to note that in other languages and cultures, the term 'austerity' has different implications. For example, in Germany, Greece, China and Italy it has a positive meaning, referring to simplicity, frugality, sobriety, whereas in the UK, the Netherlands and France it is regarded as being puritanical and severe. There is a potentially positive way of looking at austerity, where other things in life that we value (family, friends, creativity, stillness, helping others) fill the hole that consumerism has filled. The failure of the austerity approach, though, is that the cuts made in its name fall hardest on the poorest and most vulnerable in society, and the pursuit of growth at all costs can lead to the 'unfettering' of large businesses at the cost of worker protection, local economic resilience and diversity.

The 'New Deal', which we hear a lot less about but which is usually presented as the only alternative to austerity, recognises that we need to roll up our sleeves and do something proactive about our situation, that we need to protect the most vulnerable in society, and also that we need to invest what remaining financial reserves we have in the creation of a society more appropriate to the future we are moving into. As Howard Reed of Landman Economics and Tom Clark point out, "Today, our [the UK's] national debt is significantly lower than Japan's (about 200% of GDP), and comparable to Germany's (83%) and the US's (80%). By international or historical standards, the national debt is not high."[4]

But, as we shall see, assuming that we can look back at how easy it was to service debts at times of ongoing economic growth, and extrapolate from that, might well be a dangerous gamble. I'd argue that a unique convergence of issues strongly suggests that this is really not a sensible time to be deeply indebted. Also, both the New Deal and Austerity approaches fail to recognise the climate-change impacts of creating new infrastructure, 'green' or otherwise, and make unrealistic assumptions about the amount and quality of energy that will be available into the future – the energy that makes most economic activity possible. Both approaches bring to mind for me a TV hospital drama where a patient has died and the medical team are trying to revive him with those electric paddle things where you have to shout "clear!" loudly before you use them. Economic growth is coming up against some very real constraints. For example, Dr Tim Morgan of Tullett Prebon, a FTSE 250 company, has argued powerfully that:

> . . . the critical relationship between energy production and the energy cost of extraction is now deteriorating so rapidly that the economy as we have known it for more than two centuries is beginning to unravel.[5]

He adds that when the amount of energy expended in order to maintain our access to useful energy passes a certain point – a point, he argues, that we have very nearly reached – "our consumerist way of life is over".

Any approach that explicitly questions assumptions around economic growth remains distinctly at odds with what is currently being pushed by our leaders, so my argument here is that it is vital that we, as individuals and as communities, take the lead in showing what is appropriate in the face of these extraordinary times, and what a future based on more realistic assumptions might look like. Inherent within that approach are huge opportunities for creativity and entrepreneurship. While the concept of a 'Green New Deal' has much going for it, if it is based on the thinking that it will allow us to get back to economic growth as we previously enjoyed it, then I would argue that it has a huge, if not fatal, flaw at its heart. But why?

The New Normal

A lot of opportunity is going to arrive in the next 20 years disguised as loss.
Dr Martin Shaw[6]

The thing with change is that when we're in the middle of it, it doesn't really look like change. It's only when we pause and look backwards that we see the scale of what's afoot. But things are changing so fast at the moment that we could think of the times we live in as being like a 'New Normal', where what we expect from the future is already significantly different from what we expected three or four years ago.

It's in the rising cost of your weekly shopping, the fuel for your car or your energy bills; in the unusual weather around you; in the amount of money that was given to bail out the banks. Or perhaps you have a deeper sense that something is shifting – that,

Street sign spotted by the author.

beyond your control, things are rearranging themselves in new and not altogether pleasing ways. José Martín, whom you'll hear more from later and who has been coordinating a response to this in his community in Spain, puts it like this: "People feel there is a big shift happening, but they don't know what it is a shift to." I think there are three key areas of this:

1. The New Energy Normal
2. The New Climate Normal
3. The New Economic Normal

The 'New Energy Normal'

You know, the world's not running out of oil. There's all kinds of oil left in all kinds of places. We're never going to run out of oil. But what the world is going to run out of, indeed, what the

world has already run out of, is the oil you can afford to burn.
**Jeff Rubin, energy expert & former chief economist, CIBC
World Markets**[7]

Rising and volatile energy prices are affecting all aspects of our lives. The abundant and cheap energy that has characterised most of the last 150 years is over. Bar a couple of blips, every successive year until recently was characterised by having access to more energy than the previous one. Not any more. Oil production, for example, has been largely on a plateau since 2005 as the world has come up against very real supply constraints.

Half of the world's petroleum comes from just 110 giant oil fields, and there are over 70,000 oil fields in the world. Of the 20 largest, 16 are seeing their production in terminal decline. Most of those 110 fields were discovered in the 1930s or 1940s and are getting very tired. Globally, production from existing fields is declining at 4 per cent a year, and just to maintain current production we need to find 3 million new barrels of production per day – the equivalent of a new Saudi Arabia every four years.[8] And we're not finding it.

Conventional oil production peaked in 2006:[9] we have seen the end of the Age of Cheap Fossil Fuels. We are now in the Age of Extreme Energy,[10] where tar sands, deep water production and gas fracking – what are known as 'unconventional' sources, with their environmental impacts and high carbon footprints – are considered a reasonable price to pay for continued access to fossil fuels. We are having to work a lot harder to get lower-grade fossil fuels from increasingly inaccessible places at an ever-greater cost. We are having to put more and more energy in to get less and less energy out. It is a reliance on the unreliable that does nothing other than make us increasingly vulnerable, and prolongs the carbon-intensive activities that we can no longer afford.

There are alternatives, but political support is still largely going to fossil fuels rather than renewables,[11] with the world spending an estimated $509 billion every year subsidising the fossil fuel industry.[12] In spite of the huge energy potential from wind, tides and the sun, the new renewable economy is proving frustratingly slow to emerge; indeed, the UK and other regions stand on the verge of a new 'dash for gas', built on the 'fracking' of shale gas, hailed by many as the Golden Age of Gas but in reality more like a fossil fuels' retirement party.[13] We cling to fossil fuels, with all their negative impacts.

The New Energy Normal is characterised by:

- Oil prices generally between $90 and $120 a barrel, with volatile upward spikes
- Rising energy bills
- Increasing uncertainty about the future of supplies
- More energy coming from 'unconventional' fossil fuels, which require more energy to produce while yielding less useful energy
- More conflict over access to fossil fuel reserves
- Little, if any, growth in oil supply[14]
- Oil prices creating a glass ceiling to economic growth in OECD countries.[15]

The 'New Climate Normal'

The door is closing. I am very worried. If we don't change direction now on how we use energy, we will end up beyond what scientists tell us is the safe minimum [for climate safety]. The door will be closed forever.
Fatih Birol, International Energy Agency[16]

2012 was the year of extreme weather. The UK had the worst summer anyone can remember, which began with the driest spring for over a century, followed by the wettest documented April to June and the wettest summer since 1776.[17] At the same time, the US had one of the hottest summers on record and a severe drought, second only to the Dust Bowl of the 1930s, leading to 50 per cent of US states being declared disaster areas. Brazil experienced floods and landslides, Australia had massive floods, the Sahel suffered devastating droughts, heavy rains and flooding led to 5 million people being evacuated in China, two weeks of rain fell in one day on Manila, flooding half of the city, and 60,000 homes in eastern China were damaged by typhoons.[18] And then, of course, there was Hurricane Sandy.

Although we can't say categorically that these extremes are caused by climate change, it is entirely consistent with what we would expect to see as the world's climate warms. I asked Kevin Anderson, Deputy Director of the UK Tyndall Centre (one of the leading centres of climate change research), whether if the world had remained at 280 parts per million concentration of CO_2 in the atmosphere (the level prior to the start of the Industrial Revolution – at the time of going to print it has just passed 400ppm) it would be much less likely that we'd be seeing such extreme weather:

> Yes, I think that would be a fair comment. It would be *much less likely*. We are starting now to see events that it's difficult to explain in terms of normal probabilities. We get extreme weather events, we always have had such events; extremes do occur. But if extremes start to occur regularly they're no longer extremes, and what you're then seeing is not a weather extreme, you're seeing change in the climate.[19]

At the moment, the steps we are taking to reduce our carbon emissions aren't even coming close to what is needed. Pricewater-houseCoopers recently stated that "even doubling our current rate of decarbonisation would still lead to emissions consistent with 6 degrees of warming by the end of the century".[20] Although emissions are falling modestly in the West, those falls are being far outstripped by increases from emerging economies such as India and China. (Although it should be noted that a significant proportion of those increases are linked to the manufacture of goods for export to wealthier nations which outsource most of their manufacturing.)

Can we talk about a New Normal in relation to our changing climate? The consensus seems to be that any 'new normal' will be defined by an increase in extreme weather and by its sheer unpredictability.[21] As UN Secretary-General Ban Ki-moon told the 2012 Doha climate summit, "The abnormal is the new normal."[22] Kevin Anderson also feels that to talk of a 'new normal' for climate change would be to miss the point. If there were to be a new normal, he says:

> It would probably be a very short normal; I don't think this is the normal at all. It's the normal for today, but I think the rate of increase of emissions, and there is no sign at all of that rate significantly coming down, would suggest that we'll be reaching a new normal, and then another new normal, and then another new normal.

So what would be an appropriate response? Anderson argues that avoiding global warming of 2°C requires nothing less than the world's wealthier nations reducing their carbon emissions by 10 per cent per year, starting today. This ought to really focus the mind, in terms of how we need to 'front-load' these cuts. Things that will emit a lot of carbon now in order to save more later no longer seem appropriate. So what other things are appropriate, or not appropriate, in this context, and how might this affect how we plan for the economy of the next 5–10 years? An outline is given in the table below.

How the need to cut carbon now, rather than later, affects our choices	
Appropriate	**Not appropriate**
• A huge push for energy conservation; domestic retrofitting. • Sustainability criteria to be overriding requirements for all grants and loans. • A shift of emphasis in farming practices that acknowledges that well-managed soils can be a carbon sink. • A moratorium on all new large-scale developments that increase carbon emissions (airports, out-of-town shopping zones, etc.). • A rapid shift to using local, natural materials (timber, straw, hemp) in new-build housing so as to lock up more carbon than is released. • Carbon taxes. • Use spare capacity for housing (renovating derelict and poor housing), where appropriate, in preference to building new housing. • Reduce the need to travel, through a variety of approaches and support for public transport and cycling.	• Nuclear power – wouldn't be built in time, and is extremely carbon-intensive in construction, never mind the ongoing energy requirements of keeping the waste safe and of decommissioning. • New roads. • A new 'dash for gas' based on gas fracking, which reaffirms a dependence on fossil fuels rather than weaning us off them. • The continuing centralisation of public services such as schools and hospitals, which increase efficiency, but also increase carbon emissions and car dependency. • Out-of-town shopping zones and suburban sprawl, which increase car dependency.

This perspective profoundly challenges our notions of economic growth, and is historically unprecedented. But it is infinitely preferable to the consequences of a 6°C rise in global temperature. Summing up its analysis of where we go from here, a PricewaterhouseCoopers report, *Too late for two degrees?*,[23] is clear: "business-as-usual is not an option".

Put simply . . .

According to Bill McKibben,[24] founder of climate campaign 350.org, there are three numbers that define the science on climate change. They are:

- **2°C.** The increase in temperature we must avoid if we are to avoid catastrophic climate change.
- **565 gigatons.** The amount of carbon dioxide we can still release into the atmosphere in order to avoid going beyond 2°C.
- **2,795 gigatons.** The amount of carbon dioxide that would be released if we burned all the reserves of fossil fuels that we know for sure are available for us to burn should we choose to.

Put simply, roughly four-fifths of our known reserves of fossil fuels need to stay in the ground.

The 'New Economic Normal'

This is the most serious financial crisis we've seen at least since the 1930s, if not ever.
Mervyn King, Governor, Bank of England (October 2011)[25]

In the UK (although this book has a global focus, I'll start in the place I know best), as a response to the huge debt crisis, government cuts are hitting the poorest in our society; those who are

> "At present, we are stealing the future, selling it in the present, and calling it GDP. We can just as easily have an economy that is based on healing the future instead of stealing it."
> **Paul Hawken**[26]

struggling to get a job, heat their homes, afford a roof over their heads and raise a family. Services are being cut. The fabric that supports us is starting to unravel, as that debt crisis starts to spread. In parts of southern Europe and elsewhere, things are altogether darker still, with soaring unemployment and austerity having disastrous social impacts. Greece, for example, has seen a 40 per cent decrease in expenditure on health care over the past three years, with catastrophic results that were described by a speaker from the Panhellenic Medical Association at a conference I recently attended as a "humanitarian crisis". Trades unions are urging hospital doctors to disobey government orders to stop treating immigrants and people without health insurance.

Recent scandals in the banking industry and offshore banking, where large companies and wealthy individuals avoid paying taxes in the countries where they live or are economically active by shifting their money 'offshore',[27] give us a flavour of where our money can end up going if we lose control of it. The much-promised 'trickle-down' economy turns out to be a 'hoover-up' economy.

One thing I've realised is that if you want to avoid tax havens, the best way to do it is to go and live in a cave somewhere,

because they're everywhere. You can't avoid it. All the multina-
tionals on the high street that you see will be using tax havens
in one way or another for various different reasons. The banks,
of course, all of them are massively steeped in tax havens.
Nicholas Shaxson, author of *Treasure Islands*[28]

The Occupy movement has been a remarkable grassroots response
to the economic crisis and to the massive transfer of wealth from
the poor to the rich that followed the economic crisis of 2008. A
senior Bank of England official recently said "Occupy have been
successful in their efforts to popularise the problems of the global
financial system for one very simple reason. They are right."[29]

Richard Heinberg, author of *The End of Growth*, has argued that the
combination of the end of the age of cheap oil, the vast mountains
of debt that we have incurred, diminishing returns from the economic impacts of new technologies and the increasing costs of the
impacts of climate change will mean that economic growth as we
have known it is now a thing of the past. Yet still our leaders are
obsessed with recreating growth in the same form in which we had
it until recently, in spite of all of the gathering indicators that this
might not be the most sensible path to pursue.

The New Economics Foundation, an 'independent think-and-do
tank that inspires and demonstrates real economic well-being',
argues that any kind of sustained economic growth will lead to
rising fuel prices, which will, in turn, dampen any growth:

As growth in oil production slows and global demand con-
tinues to rise, sustained high oil prices and price spikes will
have a significant impact on the economy, in effect placing a
glass ceiling on recovery of the economy.
New Economics Foundation[30]

Dealing with climate change on the scale demanded also makes economic growth look like a decidedly out-of-date idea:

> We're saying we need nearer 10 per cent per annum [cuts in carbon emissions], and this is something we need to be doing *today*. We can draw a very clear conclusion from this, that in the short-to-medium term the way for the wealthy parts of the world to meet their obligations to 2°C is to cut back very significantly on consumption. That would therefore mean in the short-to-medium term a reduction in our economic activity, i.e. we could not have economic growth.
> **Kevin Anderson, Tyndall Centre for Climate Change Research**[31]

Our New Economic Normal will most likely be a place where:[32]

- Savers will have to get used to receiving little interest on their savings.
- Economies will struggle to grow and will, more likely, experience sustained contraction.
- The gap between rich and poor will continue to grow.
- We'll see 'bubbles' in prices of houses and other assets in certain places, driven not by local buying and selling but by rich investors seeking returns.
- Bank lending will continue to contract.
- Young people will grow increasingly resentful at the hand they've been dealt economically, as expressed by movements such as Occupy and others.
- Rising salaries in Asia and volatile energy prices will lead to some manufacturing returning to the US and Europe.
- Food (and other commodities) prices will continue to rise, or be subject to increasing volatility, which will squeeze living standards.

Local and resilient: the new Big Idea

Businesses whose DNA is enmeshed with the local community bring more benefits. They provide not just the goods that they sell, but the social glue that holds communities together. They provide the financial resources from which vibrant, diverse and therefore more resilient communities can grow. Thirdly, they give a sense of place, of distinctiveness, of uniqueness.

Andrew Simms, New Economics Foundation[33]

I'd like to suggest a third approach, a new Big Idea for our times, which could prove to be one of the most essential and pivotal shifts in thinking in recent times. It is the idea of local resilience as economic development. It is the idea that by taking back control over meeting our basic needs at the local level we can stimulate new enterprises – new economic activity – while also reducing our oil dependency and carbon emissions and returning power to the local level. It is an idea that we will go on to see in action around the world, being driven from the ground up.

My sense is that there is a near-universal agreement that what we need now are jobs, economic activity, stronger and happier communities and community resilience. But does the current growth-at-all-costs agenda, and its belief that *all* economic activity, *all* retail, *all* business is equal and good, actually help us achieve those things? Mary Portas' recent review[34] on the British high street and how it might be regenerated contains the following diagram showing the percentage change in UK store numbers between 2001 and 2011. It's a depressing picture, documenting the decimation of local, independent economies and the rise of the supermarket.

Since 2001, the number of superstores in the UK has grown by 35%, while all other forms of grocery outlet have declined.

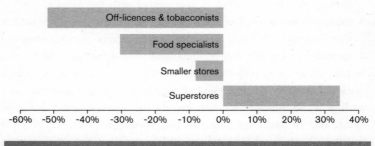

From: Department for Business, Innovation and Skills / Genecon and Partners (2011) Understanding High Street Performance, citing Verdict Research (2011) UK Town Centre Retailing.

Eight thousand supermarket outlets now account for over 97 per cent of total grocery sales in the UK; a pattern increasingly replicated in other parts of the world. It's a trend that former Tesco boss Sir Terry Leahy recently called "part of progress", describing small shops as "medieval".[35] However, a wealth of research now tells us that the benefits of more local, independent economies are distinctly different from those of more corporate, chain-store retailers.

For example, a study by the Federation of Small Businesses in Scotland[36] found that large supermarket developments led to a decrease in the number of conventional retailers in the town centre, an increase in the number of vacant units and a significant decline in the level of business activities undertaken by existing retailers. A study by Civic Economics in Salt Lake City, Utah[37] compared independent retailers and restaurants with retail chains and national restaurant chains: the local retailers returned 52 per cent of their revenue to the local economy as opposed to 14 per cent for chains, and local restaurants recirculated 79 per cent of their revenue locally, as opposed to 30 per cent for chains.

A study focusing on New Orleans[38] compared 179,000 square feet of retail space that is home to 100 independent businesses to the same-sized space that is home to a single supermarket. The former generated $105 million in sales with $34 million staying in the local economy, while the latter generated $50 million in sales with just $8 million staying locally, and necessitated 300,000 square feet of parking space. Another study[39] looked at 2,953 US counties, both rural and urban, and found that the ones with a larger density of small, locally owned businesses had experienced higher per capita income growth, whereas those with higher levels of chain businesses had experienced a negative impact on income growth. They note that "opening a single Wal-Mart store lowers the average retail wage in the surrounding county by 0.5-0.9 per cent".

Back in the UK, the National Retail Planning Forum, in a report which was, ironically, partly funded by supermarkets, found that every time a large supermarket opens, on average 276 local jobs are lost; an impact that can be felt "up to 15km away".[40] So, if chain businesses are a less efficient way of creating jobs and generating local employment, how about their ability to produce stronger and happier communities? One striking extensive study from the US in 2006[41] found that communities that had large supermarkets had less of the non-profit-making groups and organisations that build social capital (such as political, religious and business groups). The report even linked the presence of large supermarkets with lower voter turnout at elections! They hypothesise that the drop in community cohesion is due to the disappearance of local businesses, which perform a vital function in providing 'community glue'.

It seems we are stuck on a conveyor belt towards something that doesn't work and doesn't meet our needs, and which centralises wealth and power away from our communities. As the New Economics Foundation put it:

> The problem is that consumers themselves lament the loss of local shops, yet are caught in a vicious circle where choice and price, work and travel patterns, brands and advertising, all conspire to undermine the desire for a vibrant local economy.[42]

In a local and resilient economy, we regard the money that leaks out of our local economy as a missed opportunity. A growing percentage of the money that pours out through supermarkets, online shopping and energy bills instead stays locally, generating training opportunities, new businesses, new investment opportunities and new livelihoods, strengthening the existing economy and enabling all manner of new creative ideas to come to fruition: in short, meeting our needs better. It is a shortening of the distance between producer and consumer, and therefore also a vital part of reducing our oil dependency and carbon emissions. It is easy to see how this concept applies to food, but if we expand it to also cover building materials, energy generation and other key aspects of our local economies, then we start to see a huge potential.

In this way of looking at things, we start by recognising that we need to live within certain constraints, but that doing so could be the making of us, and indeed that it is in figuring out what this post-growth economy will look like that the real energy, creativity and dynamism lies. It acknowledges that we can be hugely brilliant and insightful, but that we need to apply those gifts to a future that will look very different from our past. We can, after all, create any kind of world we want to, just so long as it fits within the constraints outlined in the 'New Normal' above.

In what we might call the Transition story (you'll hear more in Chapter Two about what people are doing to make this happen), we replace the goal of economic growth with a goal of well-being, of happiness, of community and connectedness. It is an approach that will meet the needs for jobs, economic activity, stronger and happier communities and community resilience better than where we appear to be headed at present. But in our daily experience we have been moving further and further away from it, so that it becomes more difficult to imagine. I hope the following story might help to bring it to life for you.

The Market of Hope

The mention above of the 179,000 square feet of retail space in New Orleans reminds me of a recent visit I made to El Mercado de la Esperanza, or 'The Market of Hope' in Santander on the northern coast of Spain: the largest indoor covered market of its kind in Cantabria. I discovered it by accident while out looking for breakfast one morning. The market was on two floors. The lower floor featured seafood and fish, freshly caught from the Cantabrian Sea. Shrimps, prawns, squid, mussels, big eel-like things, plaice, salmon, tuna, sardines, and some amazing-looking creatures that I have only ever seen in fossils. All laid out on ice, stall after stall after stall.

Upstairs was a more eclectic array of food. Fruit, vegetables, a remarkable array of cheeses, bread and pastries, meats, cakes, eggs, honey, preserves, huge hams, all manner of pulses displayed in baskets. Rather than the kind of market I'm more used to, set up on trestle tables and gone by the end of the day, this one was per-manent. It was open six days a week, all day (bar the traditional siesta break), and each stall was its own business, probably kept within families for generations. There were no empty stalls.

Locally-sourced produce on display at El Mercado de la Esperanza, Santander, Spain.

We wandered around, buying creamy goats' cheese, some beautiful flat peachy things that are particular to that area, a bag of delicious greengages that dripped with a juice as sweet as honey, some local brie-type cheese that smelled like the worst teenagers' trainers you ever had the misfortune to be in close proximity to but which tasted amazing, and some bread. I have been to similar markets, The English Market in Cork in Ireland, St Nicholas Market in Bristol, and perhaps a couple of others, but El Mercado de la Esperanza was extraordinary.

Walking round with my shopping, I was struck that the total floor space of the market was around that of a city-centre supermarket

> "For the fact is, that this seeming chaos which is in us is a rich, rolling, swelling, dying, lilting, singing, laughing, shouting, crying, sleeping order. If we only let this order guide our acts of building, the buildings that we make, the towns we help to make, will be the forests and the meadows of the human heart."
> Christopher Alexander, *The Timeless Way of Building* (1979)[43]

for a city of the size of Santander. Yet, rather than one single business filling the space to service the interests of its distant shareholders and investors, here was a model for feeding the city from which many hundreds of families derived their livelihoods, in such a way that they had ownership over the destiny of their enterprises. While you could, if you wanted, buy well-known brands of fizzy drinks and crisps there, these were generally tucked away on shelves at the back. The huge majority of what was available was locally sourced; intimately connected to the farmers, food producers and fishermen of the region.

This was a Market of Hope. It was a market of resilience too, and it somehow embodied what we all seek: to meet people, to laugh and smile, to hear local news, to ask about what you are buying and how to cook it. It built community, it created jobs, it enhanced the local economy, celebrated local traditions and culture and it was vibrant and exciting. It was a model capable of functioning through an oil crisis, through a recession, as indeed it has on numerous occasions during its history (it opened in 1904). Rather than representing a small fragment of the past that has hung on as a museum piece, it represents for me a powerful taste of the economy of the future, of how our towns and cities and their resilient local economies could be. So . . . what does that word 'resilience' actually mean?

What is resilience?

There are many definitions of what resilience means, with mountains of academic papers on the subject. For example, it has been defined as "the capacity of a system to absorb disturbance and reorganise while undergoing change so as to still retain essentially the same function, structure and feedbacks".[44] One helpful way to think about it is through seven principles set out by Michael Lewis and Pat Conaty in *The Resilience Imperative*,[45] which, combined, help identify what generates that resilience within our communities:

- **Diversity:** much of a community's resilience comes from its diversity, in terms of people, culture, enterprises, landscapes, economic models and so on.
- **Modularity:** imagine a World Record attempt at domino-toppling. If, the night before the attempt, just one of the millions of dominoes fell by accident, months of work would be lost. As a result, the people who create these things leave regular gaps, so that if one domino falls it doesn't spread through the whole set-up. Those gaps are a key feature of the resilience of that system. Rather than being hyper-connected, we should strive for as many elements as possible to be capable of functioning alongside, and overlapping with, but independent from, other parts of the system.

- **Social capital:** social networks and vibrant communities that show trust, leadership and the ability to respond to challenges together are essential for resilience.
- **Innovation:** a resilient community needs to encourage and value learning, exploration and adaptation, creating space for valuing experimentation.
- **Overlap:** it helps hugely if we don't operate completely in silos or in very centralised, top-down bodies but overlap with each other. "Messy is better than streamlined."
- **Tight feedback loops:** this means that we need to get feedback about the impacts of our actions sooner rather than later. So, for example, local food as opposed to food imported over great distances allows us to better see the impacts of our choices about how our food is grown, and means we care about it more.
- **Ecosystem services:** a resilient community takes into account the impacts of its activities on the ecosystem, rather than just passing those impacts on to somewhere else 'out of sight and out of mind'.

"The resilience frame suggests a different, complementary effort to mitigation: to redesign our institutions, embolden our communities, encourage innovation and experimentation, and support our people in ways that will help them to be prepared and cope with surprises and disruptions, even as we work to fend them off."
Andrew Zolli & Ann Marie Healy, *Resilience* **(2012)**[46]

We are the cavalry

What was set out as the 'New Normal' above are huge challenges. So . . . who might be riding to the rescue of the economy of the place where you live, putting the Big Idea I've outlined into practice? Let's cross those potential cavalry riders off in order:

- **Government?** It is very unlikely that any significant support for the economic regeneration or increasing resilience of your community will be initiated by and funded by government (which is, after all, your money in the first place). Central government tends to be reactive, not proactive.
- **Big business?** It may be that some in your community would see a huge new supermarket or a new shopping mall as an economic boost, but experience now shows that in many cases its effect on the resilience of the local economy is largely negative.
- **Wealthy benefactors?** Unlikely.
- **Local government?** They're broke too.
- **The Secret Millionaire?** I'm afraid that only happens on television.
- **Anyone else?** I'm struggling to think who else might appear on this list. Do let me know if you have any to add.

The point I want to make here is a simple one: that in the face of this New Normal, no-one is coming riding to the rescue of you or your community. There is no silver bullet; no simple magic solution to this complex and multi-faceted challenge of interlocking issues.

It is clear that the majority of the world's most powerful governments have decided to put doing anything about climate change on the back burner and resigned themselves to at least a 2°C temperature rise, and decided that fossil fuel depletion can be offset by tar sands and gas. This ticking off of potential cavalry candidates may leave us feeling despondent and apathetic. I would argue, however, that we should feel just the opposite. It is true that we are moving into uncharted waters which nobody knows how to navigate, but the ideas you come up with are as valid and relevant as anyone else's. After all, the end of one thing is just the beginning of another. The stories I want to tell in this book are about what happens when ordinary people decide that *they are the cavalry*, that they are themselves the ones they've been waiting for. They don't wait for anyone's permission. They just do stuff. Imaginative, playful, serious and world-changing stuff.

It may not be your experience that trying to change things actually changes anything. It may not be your experience that anyone listens to your ideas very much. You may not feel that you have the skills or the self-confidence to have any impact on the place where you live. But it is the experience of many people that if you start where you are, applying what we might call 'engaged optimism', i.e. the practical application of the idea that if we believe change is possible it is more likely to become a reality, then you *can* change the world around you. Start small or start big, it's up to you. Start with what feels manageable, what fires you up and what you are passionate about.

The Big Idea in practice: The Totnes & District Local Economic Blueprint

What might this alternative approach to economic regeneration look like in practice? In early 2013, Transition Town Totnes' REconomy Project, together with a coalition of other local organisations, including Totnes Town Council, the local Chamber of Commerce, Totnes Development Trust, local schools and colleges and others, including input from South Hams District

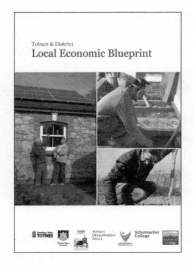

Totnes & District
Local Economic Blueprint

Council, published the *Totnes & District Local Economic Blueprint*. It was a national first, described by local MP Dr Sarah Wollaston as "a milestone in the efforts to identify the economic benefit of localising businesses and supply chains".

The organisations involved spent a year mapping the local economy and identifying opportunities for transformation and enterprise focused around the concept of 'community resilience as economic development'. The Blueprint explored key parts of the local economy in great depth, looking at where the community spends its money, with the intention of identifying and quantifying the potential economic benefits that a programme of intentional localisation could bring. It looked at food, renewable energy, retrofitting of housing and, to a lesser degree, health and care. Here's the idea in a nutshell, from the report's foreword:

> This report identifies a multi-million-pound opportunity to create new jobs, grow new enterprises and help existing businesses to thrive. It's people-based, community-led, sustainable economic development that provides new livelihoods. At the same time, it helps ensure we can feed ourselves, minimise our fuel bills and carbon emissions, provide safer refuge for our savings and pensions and take care of those most in need.

Some of the report's key findings were that:

- Up to £22 million leaves the Totnes food economy every year. Enabling just 10 per cent of this to be spent with local businesses on local produce would bring £2.2 million into the local economy every year.
- Making local homes more energy efficient could be worth between £26 and £75 million, and meeting just 10 per cent of this demand would be worth at least £2.6 million a year.
- The local potential for renewable energy is worth £6.4 million per year. A shift to harnessing just 10 per cent of this potential would be worth £600,000 for the local economy.

A concerted push for this 10 per cent target could provide a £5.5 million boost to the struggling local economy, creating many skilled jobs. It could be argued that this actually means that £5.5 million will be lost to other economies, both in the UK and further afield, and represents an unnecessary displacement of finance, but that rather misses the point.

The £2.2 million that this 10 per cent shift to local food would retain in the local economy is money that, by staying locally, would generate far greater economic benefit: more resilience, more entrepreneurship and more social and economic inclusion than if it were spent in chain businesses. If this happened everywhere (other pilots are already under way in Hereford and in Brixton, and the learning gained will be made widely available), it could well prove to be a far more skilful way to regenerate local economies than just opening them up to predatory chain stores who operate as 'extractive industries', and whose arrival usually results in overall job displacement rather than job creation. The rest of the £5.5 million the Blueprint identifies is actually new markets: new opportunities that would otherwise not be exploited, and indeed, which a bottom-up approach such as this can more skilfully access and bring about. In other words, the approach the Blueprint sets out is better at meeting our needs, both economic and social, than business-as-usual.

What might this push look like in practice? Plans are already under way for strengthening local food supply chains and promoting local food in a way that resonates with those on low incomes, promoting energy efficiency and the economic case for home retrofits as opposed to new builds, building a skills base, working with large organisations to look at how their procurement decisions could help drive this process and supporting the development of a renewable energy infrastructure.

The Totnes *Local Economic Blueprint* suggests that there is an alternative to business-as-usual; a different way forward through our economic and other difficulties. As Councillor Jill Tomalin from Totnes Town Council put it, "I don't think there is a more important single piece of work that's been done on behalf of Totnes, in any context, than this." You can download the Totnes Blueprint at www. transitiontowntotnes.org/groups/reconomybusinessnetwork/ economic-blueprint/. In the next chapter we look in more detail at how we might bring this shift about, but before that let's just take stock of where we are.

So how does all that leave you feeling?

Now is a good time to pause and reflect. You may be feeling as though your view of the world just got a big jolt. The future you've been sold by countless adverts and experts is unlikely to be the one you'll find when you get there. There may be feelings of fear – what if we don't make changes in time? What if the climate is never stable again? Or of anger – surely someone should be doing something! Or sadness – for everything we are losing, for what future generations will be dealing with.

"The cognitive dissonance we feel, as GDP figures rise, and we feel ever more tired, stressed and scared, is real, and must be challenged."
Calvin Jones, Cardiff Business School[47]

Perhaps it's too overwhelming and, like many, you want to shut down, to distract yourself, because there just isn't the time or resource in your life to deal with all of this. There's already quite enough going on, thank you very much. The problems we face are big, and most of us are not used to thinking that we can do anything on that kind of scale. When we turn away like this it can look as though we don't really care, but actually most of us care deeply – not just about our families, but also about our community, the place we live, and the future our children will inherit. What we need are tools that help us to find a creative, active and empowering response. To be able to face these problems we need to stand together, to not feel alone. And we need to see some kind of pathway of possibility – see that our actions actually can make a difference. This is a book about those possibilities.

If you're feeling at all shaken up by the information in this chapter, I would like to suggest that you go and seek out a few people whose company you enjoy and whom you trust, and make some time and space to have a conversation about what you've read so far. How has it left you feeling? What thoughts are coming up? What hopes, what fears? In other words, find space to *digest* what you've read. You'll find it to be time well spent.

Might this actually already be happening?

You may feel that the kind of shift I've been talking about is far off, but there are already some very encouraging trends if you go looking for them. Here are just a few examples:

- Deutsche Bank has shown that the global solar energy market will become sustainable by 2014, without the need for subsidies.[48]
- The rising cost of fuel has meant that in 2010 sales at out-of-town stores fell by 12 per cent as against comparable stores in town.[49]
- 2011 was the first year when, in Italy, sales of new bicycles outstripped sales of new cars for over 40 years.[50]
- 51 per cent of all renewable energy in Germany is in the ownership of individual citizens or farms, representing $100 billion worth of private investment in clean energy[51] and creating over 90,000 jobs.[52]
- The number of bicycles in the UK has increased by 18 per cent since 2007.
- The largest 300 cooperatives in the world are together worth $1.6 trillion.[53]
- A 2011 survey found that a third of UK adults planned to grow the majority of their food that summer.[54]
- 40 million more journeys were made by bicycle in the UK in 2012 than in 2010.[55]
- 800 million people worldwide are now engaged in urban agriculture, producing from 15 per cent to 20 per cent of the world's food.[56]
- Vancouver City Council has committed to planting 150,000 fruit and nut trees on boulevards and in parks and city-owned lands by 2020.[57]

- A 2012 study by Royal Bank of Scotland showed that social enterprises were growing faster than any other sector of the UK economy.[58]
- In the US, employee-owned companies control more than $800 billion in assets and involve 10 million employee-owners.[59]
- The number of short-haul flights in the US fell by 24 per cent between June 2007 and June 2012, leading to 2.3 million fewer seats being available.[60]
- In April 2011 the Mayor of San Francisco legislated to explicitly allow for 'urban agriculture' in all areas of the city and the sale of produce from urban gardens in all zones.[61]
- There are three times more members of cooperatives than individual shareholders worldwide.[62]

Chapter One in brief

- Any successful response to the challenges we face will have to go way deeper than changing light bulbs and driving a bit more slowly.

- This 'Big Idea', that local action can change the world, could actually better meet our needs as individuals and as communities than the vision we're being sold at present.

- We're not starting from scratch; a lot is already happening.

CHAPTER TWO

OPENING THE DOOR TO NEW POSSIBILITIES

As the globalised, placeless world spreads, and as progress is increasingly defined as the ability to look out of a hotel window in any city and see the same corporate logos lit up in familiar neon, it could be that the most radical thing to do is to belong.

Paul Kingsnorth, *Real England*[1]

Broadening our focus

Our options in the face of what we explored in Chapter One, as far as I see them, are to:

- Hope it will all go away. (It won't.)
- Hope someone else will sort it out. (Will they?)
- Gather some people together and see this as an opportunity to change the future of the place we live. (You can see where I'm going with this.)

The challenges that have been set out in the preceding pages are huge. Climate change? Global economic downturn? Energy scarcity? Economic contraction and rising unemployment? You may be feeling like there's nothing you can do about things like that. They are global in their very nature. They are the kind of things that governments are meant to take care of, aren't they?

Yet if we wait for governments, it'll be too little, too late. If we act as individuals, it'll be too little. But if we act as communities, it might just be enough, just in time. On their own, communities can't change the world – that will need global, national, regional, community, business, neighbourhood and personal-level change. However, my experience is that this middle terrain, the bit between the little things we can do as individuals and what we expect our governments and institutions to do, is absolutely vital – the missing piece if you like. The community engagement, the new enterprises, the internal investment opportunities, the skill-sharing, the potential of communities owning and developing assets (we'll come on to look at all these in more detail): the potential is vast.

For example, if a community starts its own energy company,

which draws in investment from local people, it may shift the way the local council thinks about energy generation and its relationship to it, as well as how it invests its money. If enough communities do this, it will start to shift how policy is made at the national level. It all starts with a small group of people making a decision to do something. One of that small group could be you.

But at the moment we're stuck. People think that governments should make the first move. Governments feel they don't have sufficient support for the scale of change required. The politically difficult decisions that need to be made in order to reduce our oil dependency, reduce our carbon emissions, build local economic resilience and so on are ones that, at present, politicians and decision-makers feel there is little political support for. So the vital role that we need to perform at the local level is to lead by example, to get started without waiting for permission from anyone and show what's possible: to model it in practice. You might think of such action as being the lubricant, the axle grease, which allows the wheels to start turning again.

As we saw in the previous chapter, the scale of the cuts in carbon emissions we need to make is enormous. But we already have the nuts-and-bolts technological solutions – the renewable energy, energy efficiency and so on, that could allow us to create a lower-energy, less consumerist society with higher levels of well-being.[2] What we have lacked are the *social* technologies for mobilising people to make that happen. The Transition movement, which we will explore in more depth in the following pages, is one attempt at creating such a technology.

If you can get a group of people together where you live and you can start practical projects on the ground which demonstrate this new approach, then what starts to happen is that the story that place tells about itself begins to shift. Throughout the rest of this book you will read many tales of where this has happened – often to the surprise of the people involved.

Increasingly, people in local government are recognising this vital 'in between' function. A friend in Portugal who brought people together to generate a bottom-up response in their community – a community whose local authority is to all intents and purposes bankrupt – told of a visit from her local Mayor. "Help me," the Mayor implored. This led to a long conversation where my friend listened, and at the end agreed that the local authority and the community needed to stick together and work to support each other, which has led to a relationship where, as she told me, "our cooperation has become much stronger, and conversations between us have become more open, transparent and non-judgemental". When the local group organised a three-day event about the concept of the 'gift economy', the Mayor provided venues and printing for free in support of the event.

I spent many years, before I started working in this direction, involved in various movements and campaigns, trying to change things, trying to shift government policies: a depressing and often disempowering task. In contrast, with the approach suggested in this book, I have felt inspired to take on change at a scale where it feels as though it's possible to actually make a difference, and hopefully you will too.

You'll be able to develop tools and insights and share them with other people doing the same in their communities. You'll be able to draw together the various strands of your community with an invitation to think about what role they might play. You'll be able, through a diversity of practical projects underpinned by a mutu-ally supportive and sustaining structure, to begin to model the kind of world you want to see, and to experience the thrill of seeing it take shape around you.

The Transition approach

> It is terribly important not to know too many rules. If you know rules and obstacles, you spend a lot of time dealing with them. If you don't know there's a rule, you just do it.
> **Beryl Vertue, television producer**

Transition is one manifestation of the idea that local action can change the world; just one attempt to create a context in which the practical solutions we need can flourish. It is an approach that I have been involved in developing. You may have heard of it as 'Transition towns', or you may have come across a Transition group where you live. It is an experiment kicked off by people who shared this passion, and which has gone far and wide, popping up in the most unexpected of places, in thousands of communities in 40 countries around the world. A useful way to think about it is like this:

Transition is an idea about the future, an optimistic, practical idea. And it's a movement you can join. There are people near you who are optimistic and practical too. And it's something you can actually do. Actually, it's lots of things you can actually do. Lots of things.

The Transition approach is self-organising and people-led. It looks different everywhere it emerges, yet is recognisably Transition. You'll find it in Bellingham, Bologna, Bristol and Brazil. It's a social experiment on a huge scale. It's also great fun. And it really doesn't matter whether you call it Transition or not.

"I see [Transition] as a wonderful combination of civic local engagement and a worldwide network. There is something out there, ladies and gentlemen, I'm deeply convinced, that was set in motion already quite some time ago..."
Horst Köhler,[3] former German President and former President of the International Monetary Fund

You can think of it as being like Open Source software. Everyone who gets involved picks it up and tries it out where they live, and is part of its ongoing evolution. Their additions, refinements and insights are available to others who are also trying to figure it out (as you will see in the 'Transition in Action' sections that run through Chapter Three). You can think of it as a self-organising system, driven by people's enthusiasm and ideas. You can think of it as being like thousands of distributed Research and Development laboratories, each trying out new approaches, but networked so that when good ideas emerge, they can be rapidly disseminated and replicated. Here's a taste of the kinds of things they do.

A taste of Transition in practice

We'll see more examples of what this looks like in practice as we go deeper into the book, but for now, here are four tasters of what Transition can look like on the ground. They give a sense of the diversity of the projects people get up to and the sort of impact they can have.

Transition Streets The idea of Transition Town Totnes' 'Transition Streets' initiative is simple. You get out on your street, knock on doors, and get six to ten of your neighbours to agree to meet seven times, in each other's houses. Each household gets a workbook full of tips and ideas, and each week has a theme (water, energy, food, transport, etc.). In Totnes, on average, each of the almost 700 households who have taken part have saved 1.3 tonnes of CO_2 (around £600), but in a survey, the key benefit most participants reported was "getting to know my neighbours". Transition Streets won the 2011 Ashden Award for Behaviour Change. It models an approach which brings communities closer together and where the carbon reduction is an almost accidental by-product. It is a powerful tool for building community resilience, and has been taken up in many places. You can now do it where you live too.

See www.transitionstreets.org

"When I came back from hospital, heavily sedated, and I had to sign that I would have somebody with me for 12 hours when I came back, they took it in turns to be here with me. And maybe if it hadn't have been for the group it would have felt more difficult to ask them."
A Transition Streets participant, Totnes[4]

Roughly one third of participating households installed solar photovoltaics. *Credit: Lou Brown*

Left: One of the groups share a meal together. *Credit: Andrew Aitchison.* Right: The Follaton Community Cinema grew out of a Transition Streets Group. *Credit: Martin Foster*

The Malvern Gasketeers The town of Malvern has 104 Victorian gas lamps, all listed, and part of the town's history and heritage (they were the inspiration for the gas lamp in C. S. Lewis' 'Narnia' books). They are costly to maintain and run – an increasing burden for a cash-strapped local authority. Enter 'The Gasketeers', or Transition Malvern Hills' 'Lighting Group', who, together with local company Sight Designs, surveyed and then refurbished all the lamps, with new burners and mirrors, leading to a huge increase in light output, near-zero light pollution, a 70+ per cent reduction in gas use, operating cost and carbon footprint, and 80 per cent less maintenance requirements (they are now maintained by Lynn, the UK's first female fully qualified gas lamp technician). The Gasketeers are now exploring running the lamps on locally generated biogas.

It has been a steep learning curve, and also a spur for new innovations and experimentation; indeed, it has spawned a new low-carbon street lighting company and created three jobs, as well as reducing costs for four councils with a spend-to-save project

> "We are bringing gaslight into the twenty-first century and it's taken a great deal of research and development. We are taking real action rather than just talking about it. It has been a very fast learning curve."
> **Gasketeer Brian Harper**[5]

One of Malvern's 104 historic gaslamps being given a makeover by the Malvern Gasketeers. *Credit: Nathan Burlton.*

payback of only three years. The Gasketeers have also developed LED 'gas' lamps, which use minimal electricity but produce a light almost indistinguishable from gas (already spreading beyond Malvern – other councils are very interested), and are even looking at lamps for the Malvern Hills Conservation Area, powered by the 'deposits' left behind by dogs on their walks! A problem has most definitely become a large, very visible solution, which has put Transition on the map locally.

Sustaining Dunbar, a Transition initiative, began with a strategic overview, a timetabled vision of what Dunbar's Transition might look like: its Local Resilience Action Plan (LRAP).

We created our LRAP in order to bring about the long-term large reductions in carbon which we felt were needed to really wean ourselves off fossil fuels. We really needed to look at the structural changes which needed to happen in the local economy, rather than just start a lot of projects which just tackle the low-hanging fruit.
Philip Revell, Project Coordinator, Sustaining Dunbar

Sustaining Dunbar's LRAP created a clear vision of what a low-carbon future might look like, as well as the first steps for making that a reality, all based on a survey of 1,500 local residents. Practical outcomes from it include:

• The 'Household Canny Challenge': support for local house-holds in reducing energy use and food waste, walking and cycling, growing food and making worm compost

"... a more localised, vibrant and resilient local economy, which can not only help us to cope with the major challenges that lie ahead but which, we believe, can create significant opportunities – for meaningful work, to develop new skills, to strengthen community networks and to enhance the local environment."
Sustaining Dunbar's LRAP sets out its vision[6]

- Working with the local council on getting sustainability and resilience into regional strategic planning
- The Dunbar Community Bakery: supported by £50,000 raised from 500 local shareholders who commit £50 or more for three years
- Dunbar Community Kitchen: a training centre for local cooks, which will also develop into a Food Hub (a model that directly links farmers and producers, to the benefit of both)
- A community garden in the grounds of the local cottage hospital.

 **The Bristol Pound** In September 2012 the complementary currency for Bristol city and the surrounding region was launched. It was designed to work alongside sterling, not to replace it completely. It acts as a powerful tool for building shorter supply chains that are less dependent on cheap fossil fuel, building better community connections to businesses and preventing losses to distant shareholders and offshore tax havens. The Bristol Pound takes two forms. Firstly, the beautiful printed pounds designed by the people of Bristol, which can be exchanged for sterling at outlets across the city. Secondly, there is the innovative TXT2PAY system, run with the Bristol Credit Union, which enables account holders to make payments from mobile phones (and not just smartphones).

Businesses can now also pay their business rates in Bristol Pounds, and the City Council also gives staff the option to take part of their salary in the currency, as do several other large employers. In

"Bristol's newly elected mayor George Ferguson will be presenting Her Royal Highness Queen Elizabeth II with a set of Bristol Pound notes during her Jubilee tour of Bristol today. The Queen will be presented with a hand-made leather wallet made by Hrothgar Stibbon, a bespoke leatherworker based in Ashton, containing a full set of early-edition printed Bristol Pounds. The notes feature original artwork from residents of Bristol people and notably include no portrait of the Queen."
From a Bristol Pound press release[7]

New Bristol Mayor George Ferguson (right) announcing that traders in St Nicholas Market will be able to pay for their pitches in Bristol Pounds. *Credit: Bristol City Council*

November 2012, George Ferguson, elected as Bristol's first Mayor, announced in his inaugural speech that he would be taking all of his salary in Bristol Pounds.[8] At the time of going to print, many hundreds of Bristol businesses accept the currency, 270 being set up to receive payment by text. Over £180,000 has been turned into Bristol Pounds, which it is estimated will turn into around £1.8 million's worth of economic activity. The opportunity for people to buy renewably generated energy using Bristol Pounds is currently in development.

See **www.bristolpound.org**

Transition as an economic approach

Transition proactively sets about creating a post-growth economy from the bottom up, contributing to the 'Big Idea' set out in Chapter One. It doesn't just accept that we have to grit our teeth for five more years of ever-more-soul-crushing austerity before, magically, we return to growth and can all go shopping again. I would argue that the enterprises that will drive this new post-growth economy will have some or most of the following characteristics.

They will be **localised** – things that are heavy, such as food and building materials, are sourced as close to where they'll be consumed as possible, whereas things that are light, such as ideas and software, are sourced further afield. They will also be built around the idea of **resilience**, of maximising a community's ability to weather times of uncertainty, to be as robust as possible while enhancing well-being (as we explained on page 34). They should also, where possible, seek to **bring assets into community own-**

"We see Transition towns, we see community revitalization efforts and new business forms – public-private hybrids, profit/not-for-profit hybrids, social enterprises, co-ops, public banking initiatives . . . it's enormously encouraging, and it's something we can all do . . . it's a restorative local economy – an economy that restores people, families, neighbourhoods, and environment and ecosystems."
Gus Speth, in an interview with Roger Cohn (2013)[9]

ership, to give the community more control over its future and to generate the finance needed for the wider localisation process.

They should be **low-carbon** in all that they do, appreciating that the rapid and urgent decarbonisation of all aspects of what we do is vital. They should recognise **natural limits**, that we no longer live in a world where credit, resources and energy are infinite, and, finally, they need **not be purely for personal profit** but can manifest through a variety of business models, social enterprises, businesses that value social return as much as financial return, cooperatives and so on.

Do we really need Transition?

You may be asking, if we have a wide variety of community groups and approaches already up and running, why do we need something like Transition? What value does it add?

One of the key and powerful things about it is that it encourages a more joined-up approach, bringing as many local organisations as possible into an inclusive process of figuring out where we go from here.

It provides a powerful catalyst, an incubator for new ideas and possibilities. It also provides support and a structure that can benefit projects that were previously run in isolation. It can underpin the whole process with an attention to how the group works and how people relate to and support each other, which can greatly reduce the incidence of burn-out that is often all too common in such projects. Also, being part of a wider network of communities who are trying things out and sharing their experiences can be very useful: it can feel lonely sometimes doing this work, and what you do can look and feel insignificant. But when there are thousands of communities worldwide who are all weaving their bit in a larger tapestry, it adds up to something awe-inspiring and strong.

Many of the projects described in this book grew out of Transition initiatives. This illustrates how the sort of structure provided by Transition simplifies and unifies within a community what might otherwise have been entirely disjointed projects. For example, rather than just starting a local currency scheme, it means you can develop it in the context of the food hub that is also being set up, in the context of an upcoming community share launch, and how the new market that is being planned will operate. A Transition initiative demonstrates that the whole can be greater than the sum of its parts.

The power of possibilities: redefining resilience

When God made a creature, first of all he shaped it in clay.
Then he baked it in the ovens of the sun until it was hard.
Then he took it out of the ovens and, when it was cool,

breathed life into it. Last of all, he pulled its skin on to it like a tight jersey.

Ted Hughes, *How the Tortoise Became* **(1963)**[11]

Changing because we want to

Will we, as many argue, only respond to the great challenges of our times when we absolutely have to? What I hope to demonstrate in this book is that maybe, just maybe, we can stimulate a hunger for the necessary changes before then. As noted at the end of Chapter One, 2011 was the first year for over 40 years where more new bicycles were sold in Italy than new cars. This, most

Just some of the eclectic array of bicycles outside Ferrara's train station.

likely, has come about only because many people can no longer afford cars. 'Peak cars' is increasingly a fact of life around much of the world, driven by economic factors as well as by the work of campaigns that have made cycling safer and better supported.

The story about the Italian bicycles came home to me in late 2012 when I visited Ferrara in Italy. It seemed that everyone rode bicycles. They were everywhere. My host, Pierre, told me that since the economic crisis began in 2008, people had been dragging really old bikes out of sheds, blowing the dust off them, getting them fixed up and heading off out on to the streets. For a town with no cycle lanes, somehow bicycles and cars seemed to have reached an understanding and to cohabit peacefully. I was told that it worked on the 'Sacred Cow Principle', based on India's sacred cows, the idea being that drivers knew that the cyclists could do anything or go anywhere at any time (rather than the 'Sacrificial Lamb' view of cyclists where I live). There were types of bikes sailing past me that I haven't seen since I was about five – great heavy things with no gears. As a demonstration of a more low-carbon and resilient transport system in practice, it was a delightful sight.

The Ferrara bicycles illustrate just how quickly change happens but how we often don't notice when we are in the middle of it. The same applies for those involved in the kinds of bottom-up processes which we will find out more about in the next chapter. They can sometimes lose a sense of how much they have actually done during the time they have been active. That evening in Ferrara, at a glorious event hosted by the local Transition initiative, an exceedingly long piece of string with a series of postcards attached was passed around the room, each documenting something that Ferrara Città di Transizione had done since its inception. The string went on, and on, and on, and something about physically

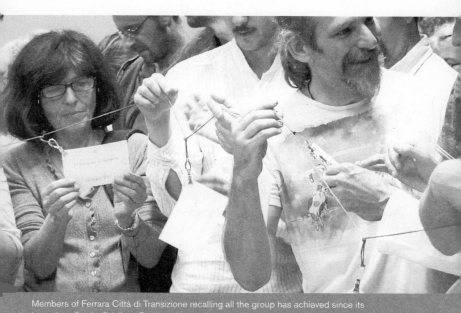

Members of Ferrara Città di Transizione recalling all the group has achieved since its inception. *Credit: Cristiano Bottone*

passing these stories around was very moving, as people were reminded of all that they had created together. They got a sense of the scale of the change that they had catalysed. There was much laughter and appreciation.

Focusing on possibilities, not probabilities

One of the central things here is a shift from a focus on *probabilities* to a focus on *possibilities*. Probabilities have been the stuff of the environmental movement for many years. What is the probability that such-and-such will happen by such-and-such a date? That we will pass this threshold, this concentration of CO_2 in the atmosphere, this tipping point by that date. While this is important work, there is also something very powerful about shifting to a focus on possibilities.

When we allow ourselves to focus on possibilities, our energy moves not only to what could be created out of this, but also to what role we might play. When I taught permaculture design, one of my favourite activities was walking with my students down a street and inviting them to tell each other about what *could be*, if this place decided to go for permaculture in a big way. They would describe the new lean-to-greenhouses, the food gardens, the vines climbing up the houses, the solar panels, the long-ago-removed fences, the community gardens.

What I am proposing is that we do much the same on the community scale, inviting people to inhabit a world of possibilities. Something that encourages and supports people in taking the step across into making those possibilities a reality.

In many ways, I think that ultimately our role is to change the stories that a place tells us about what is possible. When we started Transition in the place I live, we thought of it as an environmental process, but now, after seven years, we see it as a cultural process, focused on what it will take to nudge the culture of a place to be best prepared for times of great uncertainty and change.

Former Crystal Palace football manager Iain Dowie once famously described resilience as 'bouncebackability'. I would like to add a very different definition to this, and to those set out earlier in this book. Having been involved in the process for the past few years, and having seen it unfolding in many places, I believe a community's resilience is defined by the set of possibilities that the community believes it has at its disposal. Returning to the Ted Hughes quote above, I now think of resilience as the degree to which Transition, or some process like it, has breathed possibilities into a community, so that, as we enter times of increasing uncertainty, it feels it has options at its fingertips. Helping to generate those possibilities is perhaps the most important work we can do.

Chapter Two in brief

- To make local action a reality on the scale we need, we need some tools, a model and some support.

- Transition is one attempt to create that; an attempt that has spread virally to over 40 countries.

- It's an experiment: no-one knows how to do this, but together we can figure it out.

- Transition is a model of culture change which shifts our focus to the possibilities we have at our fingertips and how to make the most of them.

THE POWER OF JUST GETTING ON WITH IT

If you want to build a ship, don't herd people together to collect wood and don't assign them tasks and work, but rather teach them to long for the endless immensity of the sea.

Anon

An invitation

As a culture, we are currently travelling in a direction that prioritises the desires of the present over the needs of the future, happy to pass on to future generations the waste, the debt and the climate chaos that result from our activities today. It is short-termist, it devalues the vast swathes of our lives that are currently not monetised (e.g. caring for children and elderly relatives), and is designed to concentrate power and wealth with an elite few. By doing nothing, we give it our implicit support.

So here is an invitation to be part of something rather special. It is an invitation for you to be part of consigning that to history. There are already many positive trends afoot in the world: improving health care, empowerment of women, education standards, literacy levels and so on, as well as the other trends of which we saw brief examples at the end of Chapter One. How can we build on that to create a society that lives within the limits necessary to avoid tipping over into runaway climate change? This is an opportunity to shift our direction of travel to one built on foundations of social justice, fairness, well-being and happiness, entrepreneurship, the vitality of local economies, resilience, sustainability and inclusion.

The reason we step forward and roll our sleeves up and do this is because we care about our families, about others, and about the fate of the world around us. And we care about ourselves. What follows in this chapter are some of the insights and understanding gained from the Transition movement, which is just one of the efforts under way in the world to make this happen. There are loads of others too, but this is the one that I know most about.

The following are some pointers to what you might need to think about while you are contemplating whether you want to take the first steps on this journey, and some advice from people who are already doing it.

Getting the ball rolling

I have divided this aspect of the process into two distinct halves: the first looks at how a group comes together to kick the process off; the second explores what it will need to evolve into as your initiative develops.

Coming together to form an initiating group

You can't make this journey on your own – you'll need some other people too. You may know each other already. You may have met at an event organised by one resourceful initiator. You may have all been given copies of this book for a birthday and have felt inspired to kick something off. What might be some of the skills you'll find useful?

I am indebted to Anna O'Brien of Transition Hackney for suggesting the following excellent list of things such a group will need over time:

1. A **good amount of time** to commit to this and be willing to work long enough to get something up and running
2. Good **people skills**: knowing how to facilitate meetings, welcome people in from different backgrounds, listen well, manage differences of opinion and deal with conflict if necessary
3. An ability to **share power** fairly and transparently
4. Being **realistic**: clear about the reality of delivering projects, about what you can expect from volunteers and about the importance of strategic thinking

5. **Reliability**: being able to follow through on what you have each said you will do
6. Seeing your role as **initiators**: your aim is to prepare the ground for the others that follow, and you may not, yourselves, be central to the group in the longer term
7. **Experience of running groups** and organisations – how to create structures, roles, meetings and processes that take the group forward effectively
8. A **range of skills** – from managing email lists and websites to public speaking and designing leaflets
9. **Good connections** with people and organisations in the community.

You may well not have all these skills from the beginning, but you can actively seek out new people who might bring them. Remember too that support is available through Transition Training, the Transition Primer, and other Transition Network resources.[1] In Canada, Transition Prince Rupert's initiating group had huge enthusiasm but realised they lacked some of the skills they would need, and so they designed a 'Transition 101', a kind of crash-course training for themselves, which took place over a series of evening get-togethers in each other's houses, and which they subsequently made available for other groups.

You may decide that the most skilful way to proceed is to form an initiating group. Its role might be like that of pioneering plants such as gorse, brambles and birch, which you see on any degraded land but which disappear as the local ecosystem develops and becomes more complex. Here your role is to engage local people around the issues discussed earlier, and to bring into being an organisation and structure that can harness your collective energy into creating practical solutions.

Opening it out

So, back to your group. The initiating group is now meeting, you've established how you will work together, and may have begun some awareness-raising and started establishing networks and partnerships in the local community. The next stage could be to kick off some working groups based on the enthusiasm, passions and interests of your group, such as food, energy, education and housing.

Your initiating group might do this by holding a launch event on different themes and using each event to invite membership of the emergent particular working group. You may hold some kind of big public celebratory launch event, and use that as the opportunity to invite people to come forward and set up different working groups. You may hold an event specifically designed to catalyse working groups, or may actively seek to recruit people in the local area you think might be ideally suited to join a newly started working group.

People tend to engage with what they are most passionate about. If your Transition initiative is to go on drawing in more people, your working group will need to keep open an invitation to join. It will need to connect with other local organisations and put on events where new people can join. In some Transition initiatives, the initiating group eventually starts to see its role as being to step back and hand over to a new group designed to steer the whole project forward over the longer term. Sometimes this new group is made up of representatives from working groups or practical projects. Sometimes it also involves people with organisational experience, other useful skills or local connections. Its role is to create coordination and cohesion across all the different groups, while enabling them to be as autonomous as possible. If it starts to feel as though this group is at the top of a hierarchy telling people what to do, try turning the mental image upside down and seeing the structure like the stem of flower, such as fennel, with one stem supporting lots of little flowers.

In order to keep strengthening community engagement, there are some areas you will still need to take care of if you plan to hand the initiative over to new people. Developing the organisation itself – especially if you decide to try to get funded and employ staff – takes time and know-how. In addition, there are some tasks that greatly reduce the workload of all those doing practical stuff but that only need to be done once: creating a website, setting up a bank account, getting insurance, having shared publicity and so on. Often this takes the form of a 'project support' function, or 'central support' team – either volunteers or, as things progress, paid staff who provide this practical role in support of the wider work.

Transition in action in . . .
Crystal Palace, London

In 2010 Rachel de Thample's husband attended a 'Green Drinks' event, returning home enthusing about something called Crystal Palace Transition Town (CPTT), still a very small group with little more than an active Facebook page. In November 2010 Rachel attended her first CPTT event. It was meant to be a film screening, but the film didn't arrive ("a blessing in disguise"), so instead they watched a much shorter introduction to Transition and met in smaller groups with lots of dynamic conversations. By the following spring, she was part of the Steering Group, and her pet project, creating a community garden in Westow Park, was going well. Her goal was an unusual one: "I thought I'd do a little experiment to see if I could produce an entire meal myself, in

London. Why not go for the biggest meal of the year? Christmas dinner it was."

The group organised a series of films, to "keep the momentum going", to explore new ideas and to invite new people to get involved. They found the best-attended ones were where each member of the group personally invited ten people. The Steering Group began meeting monthly, doing what Rachel calls "the stuff I found really boring": setting up a constitution, agreeing how the group would work, setting up a bank account and so on.

By November 2011 the group were tired after the process of creating a constitution (but delighted that this and other vital tasks had been completed), but then had one highly rejuvenating meeting where a few new people came in with new energy which re-inspired everyone and renewed momentum. This was partly because of the several practical projects now under way but was also, as Joe Duggan from the group told me, because "we became more aware of how we chaired our meetings and made sure they were positive and productive". They started to focus on activities that didn't involve huge amounts of energy to set up but which helped boost the group's profile.

Meetings were intentionally held in venues in the community. For instance, the group working to create a local food market met in a local café, which led to the café owners getting involved and the head of the Chamber of Commerce coming to one meeting and offering practical help and support. In October 2012 the community garden won the prestigious Capital Growth 'People's Garden' award. The now-vibrant project, with its educational events, regular work parties and 'Bugs Club' for local kids, had also seeded a number of new social enterprises such as 'Palace

Preserves', four more community gardens and a project called the 'Palace Pint', growing hops in gardens and yards across the area.

Rachel sees the Steering Group's role as being to manage finances, funding and communications, to act as an "advice hub" – acting, as she puts it, "as the glue that sticks the various projects together". It also allows any gaps to become obvious and means that people are better able to see what they are part of. "It's just more about support than anything" she told me. Most Steering Group meetings are open to newcomers (not always the case in other initiatives), although for some projects that are trying to get specific things done, meetings are closed.

> "Gardening is the most defiant act you can do in the city."
> **From a TED Talk by Ron Finley[2]**

New working groups have formed: a Waste Group came from someone who had been following CPTT on Facebook, and a Transport Group from someone who had come to a number of CPTT events and had been thinking about it for a while. 'Palace Power' is seeking to create a community solar energy company modelled on the nearby Brixton Energy (see page 126) and 'Local and Fair' is working to raise awareness of Fairtrade and supporting local businesses. And yes, Rachel did produce her Christmas dinner, although, after the dreadful summer of 2012, the carrots were rather small.

Scale and focus

What's the best scale to do this on? Would the best approach be just to focus your energy on your own street? Or would your neighbourhood be best? Or your whole city? It is entirely up to you. What feels like a manageable scale – a scale on which you feel you can make things happen? This is an important question to think about if you are to make the best use of your time and energy.

What is the recognisable identity of the place you live? Perhaps, as a model designed to work on a neighbourhood scale, the experience of Transition groups on the ground might be helpful here. In London there are over 40 Transition initiatives, working on the scale of their neighbourhoods, but 'Transition London' exists only as an informal network. I asked a few people involved in Transition for their thoughts on this question. Sarah Stewart is engaged in efforts to set up a Transition group in Meadowbank in Edinburgh. She told me "I think that local means local, like ward-local, bump-into-your-fellow-Transitioners-at-your-local local." For her, the thing that defines such an area is that it is walkable from one side to the other. Jo Homan of Transition Finsbury Park in London told me she favoured using existing political boundaries, saying "there's a good logic to political boundaries if they more or less coincide with the local neighbourhood". Rachel Bodle of Downham & Villages in Transition said that in her community the local initiatives worked well, but that having a formal connection to the other initiatives in her city really helped, giving a great sense of feeling connected to a wider movement.

How might something like Transition work on the scale of a vast, sprawling megacity like Los Angeles? Joanne Poyourow has been among those grappling with that question for the last four years. Initially Transition emerged across L.A. through a Transition Los

Angeles city hub (a city-wide network of neighbourhood-scale groups), followed by several local neighbourhood groups. The city hub helped connect the earliest activists, and it worked very well for a time. More recently the action has shifted to the local groups: as people become more project-oriented, they find they are putting a lot more of their energy into projects at the local scale. As Joanne told me, "the local approach has been essential to cultivate a sense of belonging and to create real (as opposed to online) connections". She feels that a city-wide hub will be needed again at some point in the future. Stressing that the appropriate models will look different for each location, she told me "this is what works for us and for the people we have here".

So the answer really is that there is going to be no single answer. The best scale for your group to work on will emerge through your experimentation.

Transition in action in . . .
Sydney, Australia

In 2007, Peter Driscoll found out about Transition and met up with two other people, total strangers, from across Sydney, who also shared his fascination with Transition. "The idea had exploded in our minds" he told me. They were, as he put it, "enthusiastic but clueless", and decided, after regular meetings, to try to form the conducive environment within which Transition might be able to take root. This involved creating a website and running talks, and the group grew steadily.

Early 2010 saw the first initiatives emerging on the ground. There are now eight active initiatives in Sydney: Transition Bellevue Hill, Transition Canterbury Bankstown, Transition Parramatta, Transition

Members of Transition Sydney gather for the group's AGM. *Credit: Peter Dowson*

North Shore, Transition Maroubra Beach, Transition Epping, Transition Bondi and Transition Inner West. While many of these groups are at an early stage, some are more advanced. Transition Bondi, for example, is a hotbed of Transition goings-on, with regular movie nights, communal meals, beach clean-ups, 'verge gardens', community gardens, a stall at the local market and much more. It has become an incubator for other initiatives set up by people who visit Bondi and get a taste of what's going on there. Transition Sydney exists as a network, supporting new initiatives, offering group public liability insurance, and providing a channel for grant applications.

The thrust around creating new social enterprises and making a new local economy happen has translated well in the Australian context. Transition Bondi is very actively exploring this, thinking like a social enterprise from the outset to ensure that the group is socially and economically viable as a body. One of the key aspects of Transition that has worked in Sydney has been the aspect of encouraging self-organisation. As Peter put it:

> *In the early stages it was me who would go out and help the local groups run their initial meetings and mentor them to*

some degree, and I'm finding that now that we have a number of groups around, people are getting good input from a range of sources, so there is less reliance on Transition Sydney or on me as a person. People do talk to the people who are doing the on-the-ground stuff, and I suspect that is far more valuable than talking to me.

The current thrust for Transition Sydney is promoting economic development. As Peter told me, "There is no Transition until there is economic Transition. Ultimately it's all about culture, and that's a longer-term goal."

Having a vision of where you're going

At every level, the greatest obstacle to transforming the world is that we lack the clarity and imagination to conceive that it could be different.
Roberto Unger, philosopher, social theorist and Brazilian politician

To create a positive, flourishing, nurturing and more resilient world, you'll first need a vision of what that could look like in practice. What might it look like, feel like, smell like and sound like? Everyone will have their own picture of how it could be, but here's mine. It is a future where we feel more connected to the places we live, where our settlements are net exporters of energy, where our diets are more seasonal and local, and where our urban landscapes are full of food production in a range of guises. I hope I will live to see it.

It is a world where we once again have time to talk to each other; where we are skilled, adaptable and confident. It is a place where our heating bills are negligible, and where any new homes that are built are beautiful, full of craft and creativity, and don't leave their residents with a mortgage that will take them 30 years to pay off. It is a world whose local economies are more diverse, robust and entrepreneurial. We may not be able to fly to New York for the sales, but we will know our local traders, growers and processors.

Some people would suggest that this is a Utopian vision, somehow unattainable and abstract. But for me it is an entirely attainable assembly of things I have already seen in practice. It's a mixture, for example, of retrofit projects that have slashed the buildings' energy consumption; the garden on the roof of a supermarket that I visited in Crouch End in London; the Agroforestry Research Trust's forest garden in Dartington, Devon; the best market gardens / smallholdings I have visited;[3] the most beautiful houses built with local and natural materials, such as cob or straw bale; community energy schemes such as Brixton Energy in South London (of which more later). It's a mixture of local economies that have managed to preserve their independence to some degree, and the vibrant emerging culture of 'pop-up' shops and businesses. It's towns and cities where public transport and cycling already take precedence over the car. It's a vision that is already visible, if you look for it.

There are various ways in which you might coax a vision of a desirable future out of your community. For example, some groups use community brainstorming tools such as Open Space, a great self-organising tool for getting people together to do some inspired thinking.[4] Some run events where they invite people to write newspaper articles from the future.

One of the most sophisticated ways of developing a community vision is to create an 'Energy Descent Action Plan', which sets out a vision for what a place would look like having embedded Transition in everything it does, and then works out how we might get there from here. Thus far, Totnes, Forest Row, Lampeter, Dunbar and Paisley have done such plans, and several more are in the pipeline. They are all different, but are all dynamic, community-generated visions – route maps of how to actually get to a more resilient future.

Transition in action in . . .
Toronto, Canada

Transition Toronto tries to inspire and support Transition groups at the local level across the city. According to Andrew Knox, one of the group's founders, when that work reached the point of feeling as though it had generated some degree of momentum, with several active neighbourhood groups under way, the core team began to think of what else they might be able to do. They were inspired by reading about a two-hour activity developed by community arts practitioner Lucy Neal in London called 'Energy Descent Action Plan for Transition Town Anywhere', and decided to have a go themselves. They adapted it to suit their own purposes, but kept the element of a theatrical experience with large props and a playful and creative approach. .

Participants were invited to think forward, and to suggest actions that could be taken in the next year, or the next three years, across a range of areas such as food, energy and transport. They were invited to think about things they could do themselves as well as things that could also be done on a range of scales around them. The resulting 'harvesting' of ideas was then put online for further discussion, and the workshop repeated at the neighbourhood scale. The event was very energising.

"I started to feel," Andrew told me, "like we have something to offer other like-minded groups, because there was some critical point after which we could ask our members for help and the help would come. We've got over 500 members now. It used to be that we'd put out a message saying 'we're trying to do this, please help', and at some point, our membership started answering the calls. Our Energy Descent Action Plan event was a great example of something that needed volunteers and we just had to ask. It was beyond what I could have hoped for. I started to feel like we have a good base here. I feel I have almost unlimited energy from within this membership."

Engaging your allies

A successful Transition group will need to work with, and form partnerships with, a wide range of people and groups. US Transition trainer Tina Clarke has created the following useful tool to use when thinking about how best to do this.

Start by brainstorming a list of all the people, places, networks and groups in your community who might possibly take an interest in the community's well-being. Lots of them won't be interested in the issues set out earlier in this book, but that's fine; some might actually disagree or dislike any conversation about these things. Yet all of them will value the community in some way.

Write all the groups on a very large piece of paper that everyone can see. Then go through with a different-coloured pen and classify them in this way:

- **Aware and Active** (or 'AA'): they share your urgency and analysis, and they are trying to do something about it
- **Aware, but not active** (just 'A'): they are aware of things but not sure quite what to do about it
- **Middle** (or 'M'): groups and people who aren't really bothered one way or another
- **Not Interested** (or 'NI'): they are not interested in your outreach efforts or attempts at communication
- **Disagree and Debate** (or 'DD'): they tend to publicly and/ or emphatically disagree with most or all of the issues underpinning Transition and reject the idea that any action should be taken.

Rather than feeling overwhelmed by the thought of reaching out to your entire town or suburb, using this simple categorisation will help you focus and implement your outreach in stages, so it becomes more successful and enjoyable.

Our natural inclination is to start by working with all the 'AA' groups, ignoring the rest. However, the 'AA' groups may mistake you as competition, misunderstanding your motivation. If you instead focus on the 'A' and 'M' groups, and ask the 'AA' groups to provide resources and information (because they're already set up to do this!), you not only make the 'AA' partners quite happy but also save yourselves a lot of work! Meanwhile, because Transition and resilience can cut across interest groups, you are helping the 'AA' groups reach new and more mainstream audiences. In these cases there is the most to be gained – the most valuable new relationships to be uncovered. As your initiative grows, and starts to take on more substantial projects, partnerships will make a big difference.

Transition in action in . . .
Portalegre, Portugal

The economic crisis is being acutely experienced in Portugal. I spoke to Sónia Tavares from Portalegre em Transição, who said that when she heard there was a public presentation about Transition coming up in her town she "went berserk":

> I felt finally that in Portalegre, my town, the town where I was born and live, there were people that were in need of changing something, just like me. I thought that was amazing, and when I saw so many people going to this presentation, I thought "this is it, we can do something. We can actually change something."

One of the key aspects of the occasion was that, after presenting Transition, those holding the event said "but now we don't know what to do". This principle has run through Portalegre em Transição's work (a refreshing contrast in difficult times to politicians claiming to have solutions but no-one believes them). It means, as Sónia put it, "facing the danger that we don't know what to do".

As a result, Portalegre em Transição has been founded on a principle of always turning outwards for ideas of what to do, inviting suggestions and then supporting their realisation. They have also consciously tried to do whatever they do without asking for money, trying to be "completely true and generous", embodying Charles Eisenstein's concept of 'The Gift Economy'.[5]

The 'Poiso', a drop-in hub located in a shopping centre. *Credit: Luis Bello Moraes*

One of their key projects so far has been the 'Poiso' (Portuguese for 'perch'), a unit at the local indoor market that is used as a drop-in resource for Transition in the town. It includes a 'costuroteca' (which translates loosely as a 'library of sewing'), a living room and swap markets, and is home to all manner of activities, including a community kitchen used for food preparation and preservation workshops, right in the 'nerve centre' of the community.

Future plans include a heritage fruit tree library and a new local food market. Adapting Transition to the Portuguese context has meant making the economic crisis the key driver, finding ways to do things that don't expect a lot of financial input from the community, with the ideas being implemented coming from outside the core group rather than within it. Much of this success has been focused on the strengths of the partnerships the group has founded.

Inspiring others to join you

The messages in our media about what's happening in our world are contradictory and confusing. A story about a dreadful flood may sit alongside another on the same page questioning climate science and an advert for long-haul holidays. One of the first things you might do is try to help others around you to make sense of it all, ideally in the context of creating an appetite to do something. This can take a wide range of forms, but the essential idea is to create something that appeals to as many people as possible. People in your community will be interested in a wide spectrum of things: education, energy, food, buildings, personal growth, children, elders, arts and creativity, football, music, business and jobs, going to the pub, making stuff, recycling and waste, nature or golf (although in most cases not simultaneously). Can you think of awareness-raising events you could put on that might appeal to each of them?

It is important that any event that shares information about challenging issues should include making time to digest that information with other people, and in the context of what we might actually be able to do about it. Events can be celebratory, informative, engaging, sobering or thought-provoking, and some events can be all of those. Some people understand things better by sitting and listening, but other people learn better by doing something practical, such as 'Skillshares' run by Transition Town Totnes, which invites people to share something they are good at with other people in the community. Just during 2012 this group has run over 100 sessions, all free, on skills including chopping wood, mending a bike, draught-proofing your home, grafting trees and word processing. They have found that people are queuing up to share their skills, and that it is an effective way of bringing new people into the initiative. For others, a more interactive approach can be best – events that get people up and moving around, and meeting each other.

Transition Town Totnes 'Skillshare' session: the art of blade sharpening. *Credit: Annie Leymarie*

Transition in action in . . .
Coín, Malaga, Spain

One of the first Transition initiatives in Spain is in Coín, a town of around 20,000 people, with a history of being home to alternative thinkers who had existed largely in parallel to the mainstream political culture. The first meeting of Coín en Transición attracted 30 people from a range of political backgrounds. It took a while for the group to establish a structure and find the best way to work together, but an event where local kids were invited for a day at a community garden earned them a lot of credibility and respect.

In their second year they began 'Mercado Local Coín', a local producers' market, which has been very successful. The following year they held a big festival on renewable energy, which focused on the many strategies for reducing energy consumption at the domestic level. José Martín, one of the founders of the group, told me that he has observed that "once practical things start happening that people can see and touch, something changes in the culture. It feels like something is happening, that the reality is changing."

More recently, the cash-strapped local council announced a plan to privatise the town's water supply. Coín en Transición started a campaign to stop the plans, and after one week in which they gathered 3,000 signatures and held public meetings, the council announced they were dropping the idea, and invited the group to work with them on an alternative plan, which is currently under way, based on Coín en Transición's assertion that the solution requires the input of everyone in the community. Increasingly the council is asking for the group's advice, as respect grows for their ability to make things happen.

I asked José to describe a special moment that he had found especially thrilling. He told me of a meeting they called about food and farming, where 180 people, mostly farmers and producers, came together to talk about strategies for feeding Coín into the future. He was amazed that most of them already knew about him and the group, and how people who were often quite conservative were very open to new ideas about ecological food production, local food and so on. "I felt a mind-shift happening," he told me. "People feel there is a big shift happening but they don't know what it is a shift to. I feel Coín en Transición's biggest achievement so far has been to catalyse an openness to this shift and its possibilities."

Making things happen

> I was up on the church tower, looking down, and there's this amazing hive of activity, people scurrying around, fixing the panels on. People would come up to me, saying "ah, you're Mr Church PV Panels". It gave us credibility in the eyes of other people, but also gave us credibility in our own eyes.
> **Graham Truscott, Melbourne Area Transition**

The practical projects that your group undertakes will most likely be the first thing most people see of Transition in your community. This chapter has been sprinkled with examples of practical projects gathered from Transition groups far and wide, so by now you should have a few ideas of things you could do.

There's a balance here. If you don't produce any actual projects, you may struggle to generate credibility. At the same time, if you rush headlong into practical projects without paying attention to building a strong and stable group to underpin them, the group may start to struggle. Practical projects are sustained, usually, by the energy of volunteers, and so depend on being able to inspire and excite people.

One of my favourite TED talks is by Jason Roberts from Oak Cliff in Dallas. He started something called 'Better Block', which, without waiting for permission, started transforming public spaces. He offers four very useful tips for successful practical projects:

- **Show up:** claim the space, keep showing up, put yourself forward, offer your energy.
- **Be present:** be there for your community, figure out a way that you can make things better.
- **Give it a name:** as Jason puts it, "just naming something, that simple thing creates an identity and builds pride". Examples include Transition Town Totnes' aim to make the town 'The Nut Tree Capital of Britain', or 'Treasuring Tooting', or 'Incredible Edible Tormorden' – names which contain a self-fulfilling prophecy
- **Set a date:** blackmail yourself. Set a deadline, tell yourself "we're doing this in 60 days", because tight time frames focus the mind and minimise the potential for backing out.

To these I would add one more: **Celebrate and reflect**. It is all too easy to just finish one thing and move on to the next without reflecting on lessons learned and celebrating what you have achieved. After Transition Town Tooting's 'Trashcatchers' Carnival' (a huge street carnival in 2010) they held an event to reflect on what they learned, and the most important was the realisation that "if we can do this, we can do anything", a spirit they have carried through into many of their subsequent projects.

What follows is a random selection of projects that have been initiated by Transition groups, which span the spectrum from the small and very local to the larger scale and higher profile. They all capture this sense of how change and how doing stuff can be thrilling, yet they were all started by ordinary people who just decided to get on with it. You may not feel that any of them are really going to make much difference in the scale and context of the challenges set out in Chapter One of this book, and perhaps you'd be right. However, these projects are also about changing how communities think about themselves, about lighting a spark and building confidence, and, as we will see, they can lead to much more substantial endeavours.

The Ouse Valley Energy Services Company, Lewes, UK

OVESCO is an Industrial and Provident Society that was formed by members of Transition Town Lewes. It aims to deliver a range of energy-related projects to the people and businesses of Lewes district. Projects so far have included:

- Running a solar and insulation grant scheme for Lewes District Council
- Providing energy-efficiency advice
- Creating a map of local renewable projects for people to visit
- Exploring opportunities for large-scale renewable projects in the area
- The Lewes Community Solar Power Station, which raised over £350,000 in community shares.

I asked Chris Rowland, founder of OVESCO, what drives him forward as OVESCO develops. He told me:

OVESCO has a vision for a community energy revolution and I just want to see it happen. You meet people who live around you who also want to see it happen. That drives you forward. You can't do it on your own, it's all those other people around you who want it to happen too that makes it worthwhile. It's also the connection between what you are

The OVESCO team inspecting their recent installation at Brickhurst Farm. *Credit: Chris Rowland*

doing and the other possibilities. It might not just be about generating power, it could be about owning a building, or growing food locally . . .

Transition Lancaster's 'Fruity Corners', UK

Fruity Corners grew out of Transition City Lancaster's Food and Growing Group, aiming "to create areas of edible fruit trees and bushes, herbs and salad leaves, using raised beds". Its first Fruity Corner, the 'Greaves Forage Garden', is on a small patch of ground, mixing edible perennial trees, shrubs and herbs. It has grown well, even yielding grapes in the dismal summer of 2012!

The opening of the Scotch Quarry Park 'Fruity Corner', Lancaster. *Credit: Lucy Braithwaite*

The following year, 2011, Scotch Quarry Park was begun: eight large raised beds with perennial plants in a large public park, this time with a National Lottery grant. Its intention is to "strongly connect local people to the pleasures, potential and necessity of local food production". Future plans include a gardening course and an extension of the garden. When I spoke to Simon Gershon from the group he told me: "We've turned a corner in people taking pride in their local park rather than just using and abusing it. The project has opened a dialogue with the local authority as to the opportunities for planting edible trees and plants in parks, which hasn't been even on the radar up to now. It may be that a different format from what we've been doing could be more successful. What drives me forward is the vision I have of the end result, of how productive these gardens can be once they're established."

Transition Sarasota's Food Gleaning Project, United States

Transition Sarasota's first big project is the 'Suncoast Gleaning Project'. Volunteers harvest excess produce from a local farm, wash it, box it up, and then deliver it to a local food bank where it is distributed to families in need of support in feeding their families. As Don Hall of Transition Sarasota told me:

Local produce 'gleaned' by Transition Sarasota ready for delivery. *Credit: Don Hall*

We've just started our third season now, we've donated over 75,000lbs of organic produce to this point, just from one 3.5 acre farm. It's surplus, not planted especially for us, but produce that is uneconomic for the farmer to harvest.

Don calls it a "win win win" project: it is "a win for food banks and those in need" because it provides quality, healthy food to those who need it most, "a win for local farmers" because small farmers benefit from a tax deduction for the full market value of all of the produce they donate, and "a win for volunteers" because, as Don explains, "all volunteers are invited to take home one grocery bag full of produce in appreciation for their time. This usually keeps people in leafy greens for a week."

Portalegre em Transição's vegetable garden, Portugal

Portalegre em Transição created, with neighbours and local people, a small garden on a patch of urban ground just outside the town's main market. It has represented a huge shift for both the group and the wider community in terms of their sense of what's possible. Neighbours turned out to create the garden, others turned up with plants, and tended and nurtured the garden. As Sónia Tavares from the group put it:

It's amazing. I've been living in Portalegre for ever, 37 years, and I have felt my community and my city crumble, people turning backs to each other. This community garden we created tells me it is possible to do things with other people. It is possible, we just need to wake up to each other again.

Members of the group often sit on a bench by the garden and have conversations with passers-by, which leads to many ideas for

The Portalegre community garden taking shape. *Credit: Luis Bello Moraes*

future projects for the group. One neighbour told them "we were living in this block and did not know our neighbours. We had nothing to tell each other. Now, in the morning, we have a smile to share, we talk about the plants, how they are doing and whether we will meet downstairs this evening . . ."

Transition Chesterfield's annual 'Potato Day', UK

Every January, Transition Chesterfield take over an empty unit in the town's main shopping centre. At their 2012 event, they had 43 varieties of potato on offer, as well as garlic, onions and shallots. The event was opened by the Mayor, and had huge queues as over

Keen potato growers queue for Transition Chesterfield's Potato Day. *Credit: Colin Harrison.*

1,000 people visited on the day to buy their potatoes for the year. Of the 9,000 tubers on offer, over 7,000 were sold, the rest being donated to local schools. Everyone involved in the group comes together; it is Transition Chesterfield's big event of the year. As Colin Harrison from the group told me, "it engenders a really good sense of comradeship and team effort". I asked him where the hairs-on-the-back-of-the-neck moments come for him from his engagement with Potato Day. He told me:

> The best thing for me is speaking to people. Most people you speak to know we can't go on like this. They know the oil's going to run out. They know the gas is going to run out,

however much you come up with clever ways of getting it out of the ground. That's what keeps me going.

Sustainable NE Seattle's Tool Library, United States

In early 2013, Sustainable NE Seattle, a Transition initiative, opened the NE Seattle Tool Library. When I spoke to them, they had already collected over 1,200 tools, all donated by local people. The organisers describe it as "a community-led project to provide pay-what-you-can community access to a wide range of tools, training, and advice".

Tool Library organisers and partners at their launch event. *Credit: Kevin Kelly*

As well as lending tools, it also "aims to inspire its community to participate in community projects such as park restorations, and pursue sustainability through fun projects like backyard gardens, home energy improvements and water harvesting". Susan Gregory, one of the founders, told me:

> To me it's almost like magic. It's like things just started happening and people just showed up and it seemed really easy. Mostly I've just felt as though it's happening of its own accord. I can't believe this is really here.

One of those who donated tools is group member Morgan Redfield. He donated some of the Library's most expensive equipment, which had belonged to his late father, John Redfield. He told *The Seattle Times* that he knew it would be the perfect place for the tools, because his dad "would be really happy if he knew his tools are being used by other people".

Portillo en Transición's 'Dinner by the light of the pedals', Spain

Portillo is a village of 2,000 people in northern Spain. Since Portillo en Transición started meeting, they have formed a Consumers' Group, sourcing food from local producers and growers. They've also created a community garden, have a very active 'energy self-sufficiency' group and also have a group that brings together new parents and more experienced ones for support and sharing advice. One of their key projects has been 'Dinner by the light of the pedals', an event which they have now run twice. The energy group made a bicycle that powers a generator, and for these occasions, at the village castle, they borrow trestle tables from the local council, invite people to bring food and wine to share, and everyone takes it in turns to pedal the bike to light the event. These evenings were, as Emiliano Muñoz told me, just for "party time and relaxation", but did a lot to raise awareness and spread the word about the Transition group.

Emiliano told me about the kinds of conversations that take place in the group:

> " . . . we can use a bicycle to generate energy" . . . "yes, we could do a tandem!" . . . "oh yeah, cool, and with the tandem we can power a small electric wheat mill, so we can provide the flour for the Consumers' Group" . . . "and what about collecting the timber all together?" . . .

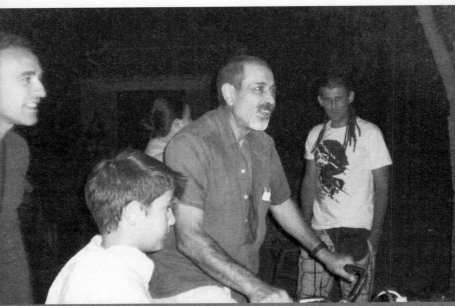

Pedalling to keep the party swinging, Portillo-style. *Credit: Emiliano Muñoz*

Transition Town Tooting's 'Tooting Transition Shop', London

For nine days in 2012, Transition Town Tooting worked with participatory artists Encounters to take over an empty shop and re-open it as the Tooting Transition Shop, the shop with 'Nothing for Sale but Lots on Offer'. It invited people in to express what it's like to live in Tooting now and to imagine different futures. Activities made people curious to leave stories, memories and traces of themselves, to which other people then added. People's affection for the area, their fears and hopes, were all gathered as the week went by. Lucy Neal, a Shop Host, said "people kept coming back, and over nine days 800 people in all came into the shop".

Tooting Transition shop: 'Nothing for Sale, but Lots on Offer'. *Credit: Lucy Neal / Alice Maggs*

Transition Town Tooting were there, but just as the hosts in the background. After all, it was a shop 'with nothing on sale'. I asked Lucy what were the moments when the hairs stood up on the back of her neck? She told me:

> Tooting Stories, a performance on the last day, was sincere, moving, honest, magical: everyone's stories woven together, like honey gathered from a hive. It made me see how very capable we are of creating the world we long for. What if every high street had a shop like this?

El Bolsón en Transición's grain mill, Argentina

The region around El Bolsón was, in the 1920s and 1930s, producer of the finest wheat in Argentina. It was home to many water mills and a culture of skilful wheat growing. During the 1970s, cheap imports and government support for large-scale wheat production led to its rapid decline.

El Bolsón en Transición teamed up with Granja Valle Pintado, a local organic farm, to set up a community-supported wheat project. Twenty-five families invested what they would spend on flour in 18 months (200kg), which was enough to buy a 16-tonne grain silo, a mill and a grain elevator. When I spoke to them they had just milled their first wheat. Alex Edleson, who runs the farm, told me:

> There was one point in the first meeting when suddenly a cascade of ideas came. We began to see the implications. There is an element in the middle, and that element is nothing more or less than the human element. The flour is kind of an excuse! What we are trying to find is to re-establish our human links. The challenge of peak oil isn't that we're

El Bolsón en Transición's new flour mill. *Credit: Comarca Andina en Transición*

going to run out of oil, it's how do we relate to each other again?

Melbourne Area Transition's Church Roof Solar PV Scheme, UK

Melbourne Area Transition (MAT) held some of their meetings in their local church, described by Simon Jenkins in *Britain's Thousand Best Churches* as one of England's finest Norman churches. They realised that the large, south-facing roof above their heads

'Let there be light': Melbourne Parish Church's solar roof. *Credit: Graham Truscott*

would be ideal for a solar photovoltaic (PV) system. The church was easily persuaded that its reserves would be better on the roof generating low-carbon energy than in the bank doing nothing.

The next goal was convincing the planners and other interested parties (the church is a Grade 1 listed building). This was ultimately successful, with more than 80 letters of support. The 10kW system was installed, and has been a great thing both for the church and for the Transition group.

With a successfully completed project behind them, MAT went on to install nine more PV systems in the area, this time on local houses, and the project opened doors for them to become more involved in other community initiatives. For Graham Truscott, relationships with other groups are central. He argues that it is the need to "recognise, praise and support whatever is already happening locally that (even inadvertently) contributes to community resilience and resourcefulness".

Transition in action in . . .
Fujino, Japan

Fujino, in Japan's north-western Kanagawa Prefecture, is the country's first Transition initiative. Hide Enomoto had encountered Transition while living in the UK, and took the idea home with him. Fujino is a small and progressive community, so the approach seemed well suited to the place from the outset. The word 'Transition' doesn't translate easily into Japanese, so they kept the English word to describe it. Initially there was some resistance to this, but people felt that being part of a network and not reinventing the wheel was important. According to writer Carol Smith,[6] "Transition Towns in Japan identify themselves with the initials 'TT', which also stand for the Japanese words *tanoshiku* and *tsunagaru*, meaning 'having fun' and 'networking'."

Two main things have emerged from Transition Fujino so far. The first is a local currency, modelled on LETS (Local Exchange Trading System), called Yorozuya (meaning 'Everything') which has around 150 members. After the earthquake, tsunami and nuclear disaster of 11 March 2011 (referred to in Japan as "3/11"), the Yorozuya became a key part of the local response in organising and sending support and donations to affected communities. As Hide told me:

It was so moving to see . . . it was a whole community project and we actually had a thank-you letter from the Mayor of the devastated city. There was such a sense of achievement when we did this: we can do this huge thing and make a contribution in our local community and we don't need any government initiative in making this kind of thing happen.

The other achievement is Fujino Denryoku, or The Fujino Electric Company (FEC). After 3/11, Transition Fujino found, as Hide told me, that "there was no need any more to talk about the 'why', everyone wanted to talk about the 'how'". The idea of a community electricity company was an inspired one: it generated a lot of interest, and has motivated many other communities across Japan to do the same.

FEC has done a number of key things:

- They powered a local festival held just after 3/11 with renewable energy, mostly solar photovoltaics (PV), after which they took the equipment to parts of Japan hit by the disaster, enabling them to hold their traditional festivals, which would have been impossible without power.
- They run workshops in how to make small solar electric systems, which proved so popular in Fujino that they now run them all over Japan.
- A local university donated 170 PV panels to FEC, and they are working towards turning a local former primary school into a community solar power station and a base for their activities.
- They are at the research stage of developing hydro power on a number of river sites around Fujino.

Chapter Three in brief

- Central to starting this process of change is a group of people who come together and dedicate some of their time to how they will work well as a group.

- Early on it's vital to work out the scale of the community your group will focus on.

- You'll need to help both your group and the wider community generate a vision of how the future could be.

- You'll also need partnerships and alliances with other local organisations.

- Awareness-raising needs to be ongoing, not just something you do at the beginning.

- It's also vital that you engage in practical projects – which should be visible, creative, playful, impactful, engaging, thought-provoking and meaningful.

CHAPTER FOUR

DARING TO DREAM: WHERE WE COULD END UP

Every time I cycle into Bath I go past one of the schools that has the solar energy systems on it. I look at it and think "I was involved in getting that up there!" That makes it worthwhile really. Generating that sense of "we can do something" and seeing that actually happen on the ground, or begin to happen, is something that makes the hairs stand up on the back of my neck.

Peter Capener, Bath & West Community Energy

The emerging new economy

Our task, as I have argued, is to build another economy, alongside the current, highly vulnerable, energy-intensive, debt-generating, high-carbon economy – one that is more appropriate to our times. I have given you a taste of where we can already see it emerging in communities around the world; indeed, possibly you've noticed it where you live.

It can be seen in the local food movement, in the explosion in 'pop-up shops' (temporary retail stores), craft breweries, the rebirth of independent record shops, the growth of social enterprises, the flowering of community renewable energy systems, and in communities taking over and investing in their local football clubs, to give just some examples.

"Transition Initiatives are quintessential examples of how localizing creates a self-supporting, diverse economy and, in turn, the ability to withstand external shocks to the global economy. Just as diversity is important to a healthy ecosystem, so is diversity in a healthy economy."
Josh Nelson, Post Growth[1]

Pop-up shops, such as this one in Bristol, demonstrate what a new, more resilient economy might look like in reality. *Credit: Ed Mitchell*

As the *Totnes & District Local Economic Blueprint* (see page 37) puts it:

> We are taking what we feel is a practical and sensible position that our economic system needs to be rebalanced. The pendulum has simply swung too far towards globalisation and corporate power, hollowing out local economies and reducing their resilience, with growing social and environmental consequences.

The shift to 'internal investment'

This new approach has the potential to change the way we invest our savings and our pensions, shifting from distant, unethical funds that serve only to accelerate our predicament, to investing locally: towards a kind of investment that allows us to see the changes it enables in our daily lives. This is what we might call *internal* rather than *inward* or *extractive* investment. The difference between these sorts of investment is as follows:

- **Extractive investment** is money invested into an economy in one place with the sole motivation of extracting more money and moving it to investors and shareholders elsewhere. While it meets some community needs, it operates on its own terms rather than taking the community's best interests into consideration.

- **Inward investment** is money that comes into a community from various sources with the intention of trying to stimulate economic activity. This investment can sometimes be used to stimulate increased resilience (as in the example of Bath & West Community Energy, described on page 121), but it can also lead to economic growth at the expense of community resilience.

- **Internal investment** is a community investing in itself. It means establishing new institutions and finding creative ways to enable money to cycle locally as many times as possible. It's about sourcing a growing proportion of your needs in a way that supports the local economy, and weaving this thinking through as many local institutions as possible – not as some worthy exercise but as the economic development model of the future.

Here are examples of each of these three forms of investment, and the crucial ways in which they differ from each other:

The differences between different forms of investment		
Extractive investment	Inward investment	Internal investment
• Distant absentee landlords choosing high-street retail tenants to maximise rental income rather than provide services to the local people • Large chain businesses sucking money out of the local economy • Developer-led 'regeneration', designed to maximise returns • Supermarkets that take on many of the functions previously performed by the local economy.	• Government grant funding through various channels • The use of various financial and planning incentives to try to attract big business to relocate (e.g. 'Special Enterprise Zones') • 'Regeneration' designed around large big-brand retail outlets • State funding supporting large infrastructure projects in order to entice large businesses.	• Community energy companies • Community share launches and investment opportunities • Investment in new social enterprises • Acquisition of assets by the local community.

Our local economies could be a lot more resilient if they significantly increased their capacity for internal investment, and this could also be a key driver towards creating some of the essential components of a low–carbon economy.

One of the strengths of this approach is that it has the potential to influence the way democracy happens at the local level. As you come to feel more engaged in shaping your economic destiny, and become more aware that your actions can actually lead to change, you see that much of the power to make change actually lies with you. This way, we have the potential to change how we educate our young people, how schools and colleges interface with their local communities, and how they see their role in preparing young people for work – perhaps with more emphasis on how to create their own work, rather than finding employment through traditional routes. This approach could change debates at the national level, when communities take the initiative and show that the changes needed are not a step backwards but are in fact unleashing huge creativity and entrepreneurship. With many people looking for 'impact investment', what better kind of impact is there than seeing the community around you growing in confidence and resilience with each day that passes?

This approach, termed 'community economic development' by Localise West Midlands (LMW), a not-for-profit group set up to explore the benefits of more localised economies, has many other benefits too. According to Karen Leach of LMW:[2]

> Our research has found strong evidence that local economies with higher levels of SMEs and local ownership perform better in terms of employment growth (especially disadvantaged and peripheral areas), the local multiplier effect, social and economic inclusion, income redistribution, health, civic engagement and well-being than places heavily reliant on inward investment where there are fewer, larger, remotely owned employers.

The new economic frontier

In order to realise this potential, we need to not just remove the obstacles that stand in its way but also be able to mobilise people to make it happen, to harness 'The Power of Just Doing Stuff'. We need a push that could be looked at in a range of different ways, as follows:

- A community-led response: ordinary people coming together to build resilience and well-being
- A cultural shift, changing the culture of a place so it is best suited for rapidly changing times
- An approach that works as a generator of possibilities
- An experiment on a huge scale around the world, exploring what a positive response to our times might look like
- A network of people all trying to figure this out together: an international learning network for life
- An approach that is not just about what happens outside us, but also about what happens within us, and how to best build our personal resilience to rapid changes
- A huge opportunity for brilliance, genius, creativity and adventure
- A model, a design for a community process that can engage lots of people in addressing many parts of the puzzle as part of one joined-up, inspiring story
- A refuge in times of huge uncertainty; a remedy for feelings of insecurity and powerlessness.

This is the new economic frontier. A recent report for the European Union on the subject of peak oil noted that "hydrocarbons offer undeniable advantages and cannot be replaced by alternative energy sources without radically changing current practices".[3]

But such radical change will need to go far beyond minor behavioural changes and reusing our plastic bags, so building such an economy – one that provides local employment, goods and services, and that's intentionally supported by the local community in terms of both investment and purchasing decisions – offers a cutting-edge exploration of the huge benefits that could arise from "radically changing current practices". Transition Network's REconomy Project[4] has been set up to provide a wealth of ideas, resources, how-tos and case studies for people interested in transforming their local economic system and their own livelihoods.

Transition in action in . . .
Brasilândia, Brazil

Transition has arrived in Brazil with a bang, with 24 very active groups already under way. One of the key ways that Transition has adapted to the Brazilian context is to focus not so much on climate change and peak oil (Brazil regards itself as the world's next Saudi Arabia), but rather on food security, violence, social justice, health and education. Those who have pioneered Transition in Brazil have also developed ways of teaching Transition to people who can't read and write. They have also developed innovative approaches for sparking Transition in places it might not otherwise get started, but in a way modelled around the principle of self-organisation.

One of the most fascinating places it has taken root is Brasilândia, a favela in São Paulo. Here the initial spark for Transition came from a group of Transition activists who ran events offering training and who suggested that Transition might be a useful approach to addressing the many challenges Brasilândia faces. Monica Picavea, one of those trainers, told me:

Local schoolchildren working with Carolina Araújo Ribiera to build a sensory garden in Brasilândia. *Credit: Isabela Maria Gomez de Menezes*

For these communities we need someone from outside who can help them just to join and then from there they go on by themselves. We try to help them learn how to do it by themselves. Transition is something very important that changes lives and places, but you give it to people to adapt. I think that is the most beautiful thing.

Transition Brasilândia has, since its foundation in 2010, developed its own identity and momentum. It has over 500 people involved, and 16 working groups. Its projects include exchange fairs, a new community bakery, a social enterprise that makes films for local people (wedding videos, for example) and a business that turns old advertising banners into bags.

A taste of where all this could go

We can start to get some insight into where all this might go by looking at a couple of the more developed Transition initiatives. For example, the UK's Transition Town Totnes (TTT), after seven years, has reached the stage of catalysing a community energy company with over 500 members, kicked off over 40 projects, helped over 700 households reduce their carbon footprints (through the Transition Streets initiative described on page 50), and created a *Local Economic Blueprint* in partnership with the Town Council and Chamber of Commerce, and with support from the District Council (see page 38). TTT is also, at the time of writing, part of the 'Atmos Totnes' project, working with the owner of an 8-acre former industrial site to create a master plan for the site as 'the heart of a new economy', and is becoming one of the key economic development organisations in the town.

One manifestation of this is their annual 'Local Entrepreneurs' Forum', which brings together local entrepreneurs with people who would like to offer support or mentoring with potential investors. It ends with a 'Community of Dragons' event, where four enterprises pitch to the community, who then, based on the idea that 'everyone is an investor', pledge different forms of support. This can take the form of time, cash, land, support, services and much more. It offers a powerful taste of what a community gathering around its social entrepreneurs looks like.[5]

Transition Town Brixton (TTB), in one neighbourhood of London, has, since 2007, acted as an extraordinary driver for an emergent new economy. Their local currency, the Brixton Pound, has pioneered new developments in terms of local currencies. Apart from featuring David Bowie on their £10 note, they were also the first place to pilot the 'Pay-by-Text' system now being run on a bigger scale with the Bristol Pound. Their innovative 'Payroll Local' brings together the Brixton Pound and Lambeth Council to enable council staff to have the opportunity to take a proportion of their salary in electronic Brixton Pounds (B£e). Anyone who does so receives an additional 10 per cent of the proportion of salary they put into their online B£ account. Businesses can now also pay their business rates in Brixton Pounds. Combined, these mechanisms offer a powerful way for businesses and individuals to support other local businesses and services, hence the scheme's tagline: 'Money that Sticks to Brixton'.

Brixton Energy is a community energy company now fundraising for its third 'community-owned solar power station' (see page 126). Remakery Brixton is re-purposing redundant council garages as a re-use centre, social enterprise hub, training and shared workspace. Community Draught Busters is a social enterprise that describes itself as "a team of individuals who are committed to the reduction of energy use in domestic homes and business premises". They have also been collaborating with a number of other social enterprises in the area, such as London Creative Labs, which works with

"This work will help us make a credible case for community-led economic development in our area. We can use the data to talk to our local councillors, chamber of commerce members, and businesses in their own language, and show them there's a viable solution to some, if not all, of our economic problems."
TTB's Duncan Law on Brixton's *Local Economic Blueprint*[6]

hard-to-reach unemployed young people in London. Their creation of a *Local Economic Blueprint*, akin to that produced in Totnes, will enable them to better make the case that their work constitutes a viable and appropriate form of economic development.

Such an approach is, of course, not without its challenges. How can it continually bring in new people with new ideas, passions and skills? How do groups sustain themselves, keep going and reinvent themselves when appropriate? How can it become something from which people derive their livelihoods rather than something that is always voluntary? Transition Sarasota in the US (see page 92) was founded on the idea that it would function as a social enterprise, providing a living wage for Don Hall, its coordinator. After two years it now manages to do this. "From my observation of different Transition initiatives, I get a lot more done than most," Don told me, noting how many similar groups struggle to make much impact when everyone is working as a volunteer in their spare time around family, work and other commitments.

Another question is how, as new enterprises emerge, can a Transition initiative continue to sustain the energy at the heart rather than it all going into the enterprises? Can it avoid becoming like a doughnut, as the energy and passion that led to the initiative forming in the first place now goes into projects and activities, rather than ongoing awareness-raising and maintaining a strategic overview that keeps watching for the new possibilities that come from linking everything up?

How can these groups minimise the dangers of burn-out among those involved? How will the initiative and the projects it catalyses stay true to the original principles and impetus that made it all possible in the first place? We are still working out the solutions to these problems. However, one of the great strengths of something like Transition is that the answers to these challenges, and the tools, approaches and training required in order to respond to them, are being developed collectively, with a pooling of the experience and insights of a large network of people.

The new economy here and now

This book has presented inspiring stories that give a taste of what is possible, but the really exciting part is to think ahead to how this might look if this were to be the case in every neighbour-hood, town and city. A new economy is already emerging – one that is showing what a post-growth future looks like in practice, one built on The Power of Just Doing Stuff, and how exciting, resilient and innovative it can be.

What follows are some stories of initiatives emerging around you that are starting to make this new economy a reality, in practice, today. They are the next scale up, in terms of impact and possibility, from the projects discussed earlier in this book. They are great examples of internal investment in practice; of community resil-ience as economic development.

Green Valley Grocer, Slaithwaite, UK

- Raised £20,000 in shares to take over a failing grocer's shop
- In profit by its third year of trading
- Part of a wider community of enterprises in the Colne Valley

The Green Valley Grocer (GVG) in Slaithwaite in Yorkshire came into being when the town's greengrocer was threatened with closure, and members of Marsden & Slaithwaite Transition Towns (MASTT) came together to save it. £20,000 was raised in community shares and the shop opened within just a few

Graham Mitchell and Jon Walker in the door of the Green Valley Grocer. *Credit: Fiona Ward*

weeks. It was established as a community-owned cooperative, and co-founder Jon Walker told me about the intensive period that led up to the shop opening:

It was so quick. We did the whole thing in seven weeks or something ridiculous, from deciding to do it, to raising the money, to doing the shop up to opening the doors – it was really very, very fast. During such a process you just don't have time to stop and draw breath, and then suddenly the shop is open! It was just wonderful and it looked great. It was a beautiful day when we opened. The Lord Mayor of Kirklees came, and it was just one of those wonderful days where you thought "we did it, we did it!" You don't really believe it until it happens! You're doing all this stuff and thinking maybe it's all going to fall apart, but just getting the shop open, that was amazing.

The shop sells fruit, vegetables and other produce, from local sources where possible. The financial assumptions underpinning the opening of the shop have been far exceeded and business is still growing while others in the area are struggling. As Jon told me, this was highly affirming:

We realised very early on that we were going to take hugely more money than we had put into the business plan, so as well as being a great experience for the community, it was clear that it was going to work financially as well.

MASTT has played a significant role in the flowering of GVG as well as in other social enterprises in the Colne Valley. As Jon put it, "it's all just happening. It's like we've created a supportive infrastructure." They've run clothes swaps, Seedy Sundays, an Ethical Fashion Show and 'Winter Sewing Workshops' and set up the Slaithwaite Community Orchard. Their Warmer Homes initiative, with £65,000 of government funding, has done a lot in retrofitting hard-to-treat homes. The Valley Wind Co-op was formed before MASTT existed, but also sits very much as part of this wider activity. In 2011, the Handmade Bakery, GVG, MASTT and the Edibles Co-operative set up ColneUCopia, a "local food brand and trading system with the aim of increasing the amount of food that is grown, produced, sold and consumed in the valley".

The Edibles Co-operative was initially set up to supply produce for the Green Valley Grocer. Using 8 acres near Slaithwaite and based on permaculture principles, it proved economically unviable to supply the shop, and so the emphasis has changed to enable it to be a viable enterprise – primarily a fruit tree nursery and a permaculture demonstration site and educational resource. One of its founders, Steve Smith, was also a founder of MASTT. As well as running the site itself, he and his partner Rosie also teach a course they have developed at the local school called 'Growing and Sustainable Living'. This is basically a permaculture design course turned into a GCSE exam, which also supports the school in its aim to become a centre of sustainable living. They feel that this is something that both supports their core business and also takes Transition ideas out to a much wider audience. I asked him what is it about what he does that excites him:

> Occasionally, when the sun comes out, like today, and when you can see what you've been doing and some of the things are really coming off, it's like a glimpse of that vision of how a local community could operate in a low-carbon future. Actually doing something, something positive, and holding on to that vision, it's very powerful. Especially if you can back it up with an enterprise that's actually enabling you to operate.

Bath & West Community Energy, UK

- An Industrial and Provident Society
- Has already installed 600kW of solar energy capacity
- First share launch raised over £750,000
- Great model of 'internal' rather than 'inward' investment

Bath & West Community Energy (BWCE) emerged from the energy group of Transition Bath. It was founded with the aim of initiating "projects that respond to the threat of climate change and peak oil, that retain economic value at a local level and that

Solar panels on Oldfield Park Infants School, installed by BWCE. *Credit: Peter Andrews*

offer people a direct say in how their energy is generated and used". It has already installed over 600kW of solar energy capacity: 362kW of solar photovoltaics on the roofs of ten local schools and community buildings as well as a 250kW ground-mounted system linked to a business park.

But BWCE sees this as just the first step towards creating a financially sustainable community enterprise able to deliver significant renewable energy capacity locally as well as energy demand-reduction projects and, ultimately, energy supply services to consumers. Because of the scale of what BWCE wants to achieve and the level of finance that will need to be raised locally as a result, a key part of its initial focus has been on creating an economic model that generates confidence in BWCE as a reliable investment.

Early in its existence the group got the support of SSE (Scottish and Southern Energy, one of the UK's 'big six' energy companies) and negotiated a £1 million loan facility with them. This enabled BWCE to underwrite a number of solar installations in advance of its community share issue. The success of the share launch took the group by surprise, raising £722,000 from local investors. Peter Capener, one of the founders, told me that "in the last couple of weeks (of the share launch) we had about £300,000 coming in, and people were going round to fellow director Peter Andrews' house thrusting cheques into his hand". When I asked why he thought the share launch went so well, he said "It was a real and genuine enthusiasm that people were expressing, almost verging on relief, that somebody was doing something that they could actually get involved in and be a part of."

The model that they had created offered, unlike many similar initiatives, an annual return from the end of the first year. From the outset BWCE aimed to offer its investors a return of 7 per cent per annum. Such a healthy return meant that some people invested via their self-invested personal pension funds (SIPPs), a fascinating example of what 'internal investment' (as opposed to 'inward investment') could look like in practice. What next? BWCE is looking at a number of projects: more solar installations, some potential wind power projects and a couple of possible hydro schemes on the river Avon, as well as energy-efficiency and renewable-heat projects.

BWCE is also working with a number of other local organisations and neighbouring community groups to provide the support they need to set up similar schemes. Peter told me:

There are three communities we're currently working with directly to set up their own community energy enterprises. They all started off with the same question in their minds as we did, which was "can we really do this?" We're now able to say "yes, you can, we can help you do this, we can provide technical expertise and help round the sometimes complex legal situations. We can advise you how to engage with your communities to raise finance and publicise your offer." That's the reason why I feel excited and enthused by this, it's that feeling of being part of a local movement if you like; building a sense of collective purpose around what we and others are doing.

DE4 Food, Derbyshire, UK

- A food hub offering a real and affordable alternative to super-markets
- Over 200 members
- Makes growing food in the back garden for sale viable
- Most people involved in the enterprise learned to run a business 'on the job'

DE4 Food is "a cooperative social enterprise made up of small-scale local food and drink producers and their customers" that covers the DE4 postcode area in Derbyshire and which emerged from Transition Matlock (TM). It now functions with 200 members, connecting its members with local food and drink producers through its online shop. TM's Food Group started trying to create a local directory, but found so few local growers that they never published it! They decided they needed to create a Community Supported Agriculture (CSA) scheme (described by the UK's Soil Association as "a partnership between farmers and the local community, in which the responsibilities, risks and rewards of

DE4 FOOD

local food made easy

Are you looking for an alternative to the supermarkets for your weekly shop?

Do you want to support local producers but don't have the time to search them out?

Do you want the option of picking up your weekly shopping or get it delivered to the door?

Are you looking for a flexible way to buy local food and drink?

DE4 Food is the answer...

Shop online with us at

www.de4food.org.uk

email: info@de4food.org.uk
twitter: @DE4food

farming are shared") and, given that most farming in their area is livestock, they started a lamb CSA. Members worked with a local farmer in exchange for a proportion of the produce. The group got their hands dirty together, learned new skills, and, around that time, heard about StroudCo, a food hub in Stroud.

Inspired, they felt that the food hub might be the model for them. They weren't able to find organic vegetable growers who could supply enough to meet demand, so they took a different approach, along the lines of a 'patchwork farm', where people could grow on a back-garden scale to supply the scheme. They feel that this model brings together everything they had set out to address: supporting people to grow their own food, learning new skills, creating a new economy and supporting local growers. The DE4 Food website offers tips for growers and sells fruit bushes and vegetable seedlings. I asked Helen Cunningham from DE4 Food how being involved had affected her:

> Never in my life did I imagine that I'd be able to bring lambs into the world! It wasn't a skill I ever expected to have. It was such a different thing from what we were doing in the rest of our lives, and I think from then we've all thought "OK, we can learn these new skills, we can learn how to lamb, we can learn

how to grow vegetables and learn how to do Excel Profit and Loss sheets and whatever." I think we all just really wanted to change the way we live, and change our own personal lives and to change things and live different lives ourselves as well as a different life in our community.

Brixton Energy, London

- The UK's first community-owned inner-city energy company
- Has raised £130,000 in two share launches
- Gives shareholders a good return on their investment
- Has trained local young people in a range of skills

When I met Agamemnon Otero, director of Brixton Energy and Repowering South London, Brixton Energy had just closed its second share launch, Brixton Energy Solar 2, which had raised £70,000. Its first project, Brixton Energy Solar 1, was the UK's first inner-city community-owned solar power station, a 37kW solar array on the roof of Elmore House on the Loughborough housing estate. The second was a 45kW system spread over the roofs of the four housing blocks known as Styles Gardens. I joined Agamemnon on the roof of a neighbouring tower block on a crisp and clear winter day, with a clear view over the solar systems that Brixton Energy had already installed, to ask him more about the project. He explained:

> Brixton Energy is really just a name, a tag. The cooperatives themselves are Brixton Energy Solar 1, Brixton Energy Solar 2, Brixton Energy Solar 3 and so on. Repowering South London does the core of the work – the financial modelling, the legal work, writing the bids, the technical modelling and so on, all that came in from them. However, the major work of communicating with the community, knocking on doors

Agamemnon Otero with Brixton Energy Solar 2 on rooftops behind him (and behind that Brixton Energy Solar 1 if you look very closely).

and whatever, that came from a mixture of Transition Town Brixton (TTB) and other dedicated local people, knocking on doors and inviting people to get involved.

For Brixton Energy Solar 1, we did lots of engagements. We started inviting people, but that was more difficult than we'd thought . . . getting people out to knock on doors, that was a bit tough. We went to the local farmers' market, we used TTB's network, everybody's friends and family, and we sent our prospectus out saying "this is what we're doing". We raised the money in three weeks.

For Brixton Energy Solar 2 we had five young people from the estate doing paid work-experience installing them. We've had local young people doing apprenticeships in finance, legal, IT, PR and technical installation. After Brixton Energy Solar 1, it just spread like wildfire, to the point where Brixton Energy Solar 2 was a huge success, and up the road another block, they heard about this, and now they want it too. One guy said "if something had gone wrong, we'd know. We've heard nothing bad."

With Brixton Solar 2, the community is behind us now. The woman who lives in that flat there, her son, her two daughters, and her friends, and then their cousins who live in the place we're going to do Brixton Solar 3, came down to do work experience. Then there was another lady, a local business woman who has stalls in Brixton Market, she invested, and the woman from over there invested.

Ten people from these buildings invested, and then more from the estate did too. In the next project, Brixton Energy Solar 3, we might be able to do it where all the money is raised from the people on the estate.

The Community Energy Efficiency Fund raises £6,000 over the next 20 years and we've already match-funded that, so there's £12,000 raised for apprenticeships, draught-busting and reducing energy consumption. Planning our first project took us eight or nine months, the second one took us three months, the third project took a month. We have 11 more sites ready to go.

There's a woman lives here, she's at the bottom of everything. She's got four kids, she's a single mum, she said "this is the best thing. I'm saving money on my energy bills, my kids are really into it, they came to the community workshops." She didn't say "I want it, I feel really good about myself"; she said "I just hope this can go to other estates". When you link all those people up, for me, the hairs on the back of my neck continue to stay up!

Ultimately, what we're really all about is trying to change minds, on the ground, and to make people warmer. Energy, solar panels or whatever, are just a way to get there. We're not wedded to solar panels, or combined heat and power, or whatever. We're wedded to well-being. The only way people believe in themselves and get involved is when they're allowed to be involved. As soon as you take responsibility for something and you give and you take back and you give and you take back, you develop self-will and self-belief, and that's what's been taken away from people.

Chapter Four in brief

- Rather than waiting for permission, Transition initiatives and others are already starting to build a new economy founded on local action.

- It's different in each place, and it can already be seen in a number of innovative enterprises.

- When you start to join up what may look like lots of small unrelated initiatives, the potential becomes clear.

- If we get this right, there is huge economic potential and untapped power that we can take back in our communities – The Power of Just Doing Stuff.

A FEW CLOSING THOUGHTS

There are roots of the new life spreading everywhere, with no central plan, but moving and networking, keeping the energy, waiting for spring.

Manuel Castells, *Networks of Outrage and Hope (2012)*[1]

The stories we heard in the last chapter, from Bath, Slaithwaite, Derbyshire and Brixton, are, we might say, the pioneer plants of the new economy breaking through the tarmac of business-as-usual. They contain a taste, a seed, of a new, more decentralised, more fairly distributed, more appropriate and more resilient economy. They offer a taste of what's possible. They are showing that it works. They are just doing stuff, but with a nurturing and supportive infrastructure behind them.

And there is a real power to that. I could sense it in all the people I interviewed for this book. There was a sense from each of them that they felt part of something that had momentum, that was making a real and visible impact on their surroundings, and that was leading to their feeling more connected to and part of the community around them. There was also a strong sense that this is the time: a time that demands action. As a friend involved in my own Transition initiative told me, "this is a better vision than anyone else has got at this stage, it's one that will give us a future".

Where could all this go? It isn't the aim of the Transition approach to create a new national energy company, for example; rather, a vibrant network of thousands of community energy companies, sharing experience, insight and support. It isn't the aim to create one national 'Bank of Transition'; rather, a mosaic of innovative and place-specific internal investment approaches, which link up and share their experience. The power of this lies in networks, of the accumulation of experience that makes it progressively easier for others to get started where they are.

Decision-makers at different levels also have a role to play here. Local government and national government clearly have a huge amount to do in order to build the kind of economy that has been set out in this book, refocusing their efforts on resilience and localisation. The big question is how they can support the kinds of activities I have described without taking them over or swamping them with bureaucracy. But the key driver must remain the people: the communities, the people on the ground with the rolled-up sleeves and the fire in their bellies.

It is my experience that when you meet the people who are supposed to be in charge and to be resolving the challenges we are facing, they generally have as little idea of what to do as anyone else, as we saw in our story of the local government leaders at the beginning of the book. In this regard, to borrow a phrase from certain politicians who really don't mean it at all, we really are 'all in this together'.

I hope I have left you with a sense of how small changes can add up to something big and extraordinary. I hope I have also given you a sense that you may well be just the very person to start something wonderful where you live. I can't guarantee that this will be enough. But what I do know is that now is the time, and that if we do this, our children and grandchildren will tell great tales and sing great songs about what we did in these most fascinating of days.

This book has been about taking power back into your own hands, quite literally in the case of the Fujino Electric Co. (above, see page 103). Whether it starts small like Portalegre em Transição's garden (below left, see page 93) or hugely ambitious like the Atmos Totnes project (below right, see page 115), it is the vital work of our times. *Credits: Kazuhiro Hakamada (above), Luis Bello Moraes (below left), David Pearson (below right)*

Next steps

If you have made it this far in the book then I will take the liberty of assuming that you may like to know how to take this further. I have assembled here some of the key next steps you could take.

- You could have a look at www.transitionnetwork.org, where the many resources include www.transitionnetwork.org/nearby, where you can type in your postcode and find out about Transition projects, initiatives and people who are involved near you.
- You could download *The Transition Primer*, the free guide to the first steps in getting this process under way in your community, from www.transitionnetwork.org. Available from autumn 2013.
- You could watch *In Transition 2.0*, the latest film on Transition, available from www.intransitionmovie.com. *In Transition 1.0* is available to watch at www.vimeo.com/8029815, and a search for 'Transition Town' on YouTube will reveal many other gems.
- You could keep up with the Transition Network's Social Reporters blog, where people involved in this process write about their experiences: www.transitionnetwork.org/stories
- You might do Transition Launch, the two-day training designed to support you in getting this under way in your community: www.transitionnetwork.org/training
- You could seek out a copy of, or distribute and support, *Transition Free Press*, the quarterly newspaper about Transition: www.transitionfreepress.org
- If your interest is in creating a social enterprise or a new livelihood based on Transition thinking, Transition Network's

REconomy Project, full of case studies, tips and tools, can be found at www.reconomy.org

- You could read *The Transition Companion: making your community more resilient in uncertain times*, published by Green Books in 2011, which is the complete overview of Transition and how to do it.

- Then there's also Shaun Chamberlin's book *The Transition Timeline: for a local, resilient future* (2009, Green Books). And it all began with *The Transition Handbook: from oil dependency to local resilience* (2009, Green Books, and written by me), which is now only available as an ebook from www.greenbooks.co.uk. See the Resources section for more books on the Transition approach in specific subject areas.

Notes*

Chapter 1

1 Maslow, A. H. (1971) *The Farther Reaches of Human Nature.* Penguin Books.

2 From an interview I did with him on TransitionCulture.org on 20 December 2011, published as *Can we manage without growth? An interview with Peter Victor, Part One.* http://transitionculture. org/2011/12/20/can-we-manage-without-growth-an-interview-with-peter-victor-part-one/

3 Barnes, G. (2013) *Money and sustainability – the missing link: review.* The Foundation for the Economics of Sustainability. http://www. feasta.org/2013/01/31/money-and-sustainability-the-missing-link-review/

4 Reed, H., Clark, T. (2013) *Mythbuster: 'Britain is broke – we can't afford to invest'.* New Economics Foundation. 4 April 2013. http://www.neweconomics.org/publications/mythbuster-britain-is-broke-we-cant-afford-to-invest

5 Morgan, T. (2013) *Perfect storm: energy, finance and the end of growth.* Tullett Prebon. http://www.tullettprebon.com/Documents/strategyinsights/TPSI_009_Perfect_Storm_009.pdf

6 From an interview I did with Dr Martin Shaw on 17 September 2012, called *An interview with Dr. Martin Shaw: 'A lot of opportunity is going to arrive in the next 20 years disguised as loss'.* Available at: www.transitionculture.org/2012/09/17/an-interview-with-dr-martin-shaw-a-lot-of-opportunity-is-going-to-arrive-in-the-next-20-years-disguised-as-loss/

7 From a video at www.youtube/U47z5pPIFpU

A set of these Notes with live hyperlinks can be downloaded from www.greenbooks.co.uk/The-Power-Of-Just-Doing-Stuff.html

8 Sorrell, S., Speirs, J., Bentley, R., Brandt, A., Miller, R. (2009) *Global oil depletion: an assessment of the evidence for a near-term peak in global oil production.* UK Energy Research Centre.

9 Inman, M. (2010) *Has the world already passed 'peak oil'? New analysis pegs 2006 as highpoint of conventional crude production.* National Geographic.com. 9 November 2010. http://news.nationalgeographic.com/news/energy/2010/11/101109-peak-oil-iea-world-energy-outlook/

10 A term coined by Michael Klare. See for example Klare, M. (2010) *The relentless pursuit of extreme energy: a new oil rush endangers the Gulf of Mexico and the planet.* Huffington Post. 19 May 2010. www.huffingtonpost.com/michael-t-klare/the-relentless-pursuit-of_b_581921.html

11 According to Oil Change International, the world's rich nations spend five times more on subsidising the fossil fuel industry than they do on supporting developing nations' responses to climate change. Turnbull, D. (2012) *New analysis: fossil fuel subsidies five times greater than climate finance.* 3 December 2012. www.priceofoil.org/2012/12/03/new-analysis-fossil-fuel-subsidies-five-times-greater-than-climate-finance/

12 From Share the World's Resources (2012) *Financing the global sharing economy.* 15 October 2012. Can be downloaded from www.stwr.org/financing-the-global-sharing-economy

13 I am indebted to Andrew Nikiforuk for this choice of words. 28 March 2013. http://www.resilience.org/stories/2013-03-28/the-shale-gale-is-a-retirement-party/

14 Strahan, D. (2012) *Peakonomics: kiss your boarding pass goodbye.* 4 June 2012. www.davidstrahan.com/blog/?p=1517/

15 An argument explored in more detail in Johnson, V., Simms, A., Skrebowski, C., Greenham, T. (2012) *The economics of oil dependence: a glass ceiling to recovery. Why the oil industry today is like banking was in 2006.* New Economics Foundation.

16 In: Harvey, F. (2011) *World headed for irreversible climate change in five years, IEA warns. The Guardian.* 9 November 2011. www.guardian.co.uk/environment/2011/nov/09/fossil-fuel-infrastructure-climate-change

17 Harrabin, R. (2012) *UK experiences 'weirdest' weather.* BBC Science News. 18 October 2012.
www.bbc.co.uk/news/science-environment-19995084

18 A powerful timeline of 2012's extreme weather events can be found at
www.tiki-toki.com/timeline/entry/55279/Extreme-Weather-Climate-Events-2012/#vars!date=2011-12-18_07:56:44!

19 2 November 2012. You can see the interview in full at
www.transitionculture.org/2012/11/02/an-interview-with-kevin-anderson-rapid-and-deep-emissions-reductions-may-not-be-easy-but-4c-to-6c-will-be-much-worse/

20 PricewaterhouseCoopers (2012) *Too late for two degrees? Low carbon economy index 2012.* www.pwc.com/en_GX/gx/low-carbon-economy-index/assets/pwc-low-carbon-economy-index-2012.pdf

21 See, for example, Hansen, K. (2012) *Research links extreme summer heat events to global warming.* NASA Earth Science News. 8 June 2012. www.nasa.gov/topics/earth/features/warming-links.html/

22 Reuters (2012) *Extreme weather the new 'normal'?* 4 December 2012. www.foxbusiness.com/industries/2012/12/04/extreme-weather-new-normal/

23 PricewaterhouseCoopers (2012) *Too late for two degrees? Low carbon economy index 2012.* http://www.pwc.co.uk/sustainability-climate-change/publications/low-carbon-economy-index.jhtml

24 McKibben, B. (2012) *Global warming's terrifying new math: three simple numbers that add up to global catastrophe – and that make clear who the real enemy is. Rolling Stone.* 19 July 2012.
www.rollingstone.com/politics/news/global-warmings-terrifying-new-math-20120719

25 BBC Business News (2011) *Bank of England governor fears crisis is 'worst ever'.* 7 October 2011.
www.bbc.co.uk/news/business-15210112

26 Hawken, P. (2009) *Commencement: healing or stealing? Commencement address, University of Portland.* http://www.up.edu/commencement/default.aspx?cid=9456&pid=3144

27 Essential reading on this is Shaxson, N. (2011) *Treasure Islands: tax havens and the men who stole the world.* The Bodley Head.

28 From an interview I did with Nick Shaxson for TransitionCulture. org. 14 May 2012. www.transitionculture.org/2012/05/14/ an-interview-with-nick-shaxson-author-of-treasure-islands-tax-havens-and-the-men-who-stole-the-world/

29 Kirkup, J. (2012) *Occupy protesters were right, says Bank of England official. The Telegraph.* 29 October 2012. www.telegraph.co.uk/ finance/newsbysector/banksandfinance/9641806/Occupy-protesters-were-right-says-Bank-of-England-official.html

30 Johnson, V., Simms, A., Skrebowski, C., Greenham, T. (2012) *The economics of oil dependence: a glass ceiling to recovery. Why the oil industry today is like banking was in 2006.* New Economics Foundation.

31 2 November 2012. www.transitionculture.org/2012/11/02/ an-interview-with-kevin-anderson-rapid-and-deep-emissions-reductions-may-not-be-easy-but-4c-to-6c-will-be-much-worse/

32 I am grateful to Tony Greenham of New Economic Foundation for his input into this list.

33 From an interview I did with him: *Andrew Simms on the impacts of chain stores on local economies.* TransitionCulture.org. 5 June 2012. http://transitionculture.org/2012/06/05/andrew-simms-on-the-impacts-of-chain-stores-on-local-economies/

34 Portas, M. (2011) *The Portas Review: an independent review into the future of our high streets.* Department for Business, Innovation and Skills.

35 BBC News Online (2013) *Small shop closures are progress, says ex-Tesco boss.* 3 February 2013. http://www.bbc.co.uk/news/uk-21310808

36 Federation of Small Businesses (Scotland) (2006) *The effect of supermarkets on existing retailers.* Roger Tym & Partners.

37 Civic Economics (2012) *Indie impacts study series: a national comparative survey with the American Booksellers Association. Salt Lake City.* http://www.localfirst.org/images/stories/SLC-Final-Impact-Study-Series.pdf

38 The Urban Conservancy / Civic Economics (2009) *Thinking outside the box: a report on independent merchants and the New Orleans economy.* Available from http://bealocalist.org/thinking-outside-box-report-independent-merchants-and-local-economy-profile

39 Fleming, D. A., Goetz, S. J. (2011) *Does local firm ownership matter? Economic Development Quarterly.* August 2011 25: 277-281

40 Porter, S, Raistrick, P. (1998) *The impact of out-of-centre food superstores on local retail employment.* The National Retail Planning Forum.

41 Goetz, S.J., Rupasingha, A. (2006) *WalMart and social capital.* Northeast Regional Center for Rural Development. http://aese.psu.edu/nercrd/economic-development/materials/poverty-issues/big-boxes/wal-mart-and-social-capital/article-wal-mart-and-social-capital/view

42 Simms, A., Oram, J., MacGillivray, A., Drury, J. (2002) *Ghost town Britain: The threat from economic globalisation to livelihoods, liberty and local economic freedom.* New Economics Foundation.

43 Alexander, C. (1979) *The Timeless Way of Building.* Oxford University Press.

44 Walker, B., Salt, D. (2006) *Resilience Thinking: sustaining ecosystems and people in a changing world.* Island Press.

45 Lewis, M., Conaty, P. (2012) *The Resilience Imperative: cooperative transitions to a steady-state economy.* New Society Publishers.

46 Zolli, A., Healy, A. M. (2012) *Resilience: why things bounce back.* Headline Business Plus.

47 Jones, C. (2013) *Technology cannot tackle climate change: Calvin Jones says Wales can lead the way in replacing economic growth with the notion of useful work.* http://www.clickonwales.org/2013/04/technology-cannot-tackle-climate-change/

48 Beetz, B. (2013) *Deutsche Bank: sustainable solar market expected in 2014. PV Magazine.* http: pv-magazine.com/news/details/beitrag/deutsche-bank--sustainable-solar-market-expected-in-2014_100010338/

49 Bawden, T., Milmo, D. (2011) *Out-of-town shopping malls suffer as fuel price deters shoppers. The Guardian.* 8 April 2011. www.guardian.co.uk/business/2011/apr/08/town-shopping-malls-fuel-price

50 Squires, N. (2012) *More bikes sold than cars in Italy for first time since WW2. The Telegraph.* 2 October 2012. www.telegraph.co.uk/finance/newsbysector/transport/9581180/More-bikes-sold-than-cars-in-Italy-for-first-time-since-WW2.html

51 McDermott, M. (2012) *Over half of Germany's renewable energy owned by citizens & farmers, not utility companies.* Treehugger.com. 26 January 2012. http://www.treehugger.com/renewable-energy/over-half-germany-renewable-energy-owned-citizens-not-utility-companies.html/

52 Gsänger, S. (2009) *Community power empowers.* Discovery News. www.news.discovery.com/tech/community-wind-power-opinion.html

53 Co-operative News (2012) *Power of co-operation: members outnumber shareholders by three to one.* 11 January 2012. www.thenews.coop/article/power-co-operation-members-outnumber-shareholders-three-one/

54 Wallop, H. (2011) *A third say they will grow their own this summer.* The Telegraph. 6 April 2011. www.telegraph.co.uk/gardening/plants/vegetables/8429480/A-third-say-they-will-grow-their-own-this-summer.html

55 Sustrans (2012) *Cycling increase by 18 per cent on National Cycle Network.* 18 June 2012. www.sustrans.org.uk/about-sustrans/media/news-releases/cycling-increase-by-18-per-cent-on-national-cycle-network

56 Statistic from United Nations Development Programme. Quoted in Zuckerman, J. C. (2011) *The Constant Gardeners.* One Earth. 28 November 2011. www.onearth.org/article/the-constant-gardeners/

57 Shore, R. (2012) *Vancouver to plant more food-bearing trees on streets and in parks.* Vancouver Sun. 3 November 2012. http://blogs.vancouversun.com/2012/10/03/vancouver-to-plant-more-food-bearing-trees-on-streets-and-in-parks/

58 Social Enterprise Live (2011) *Vibrant sector defies downturn with powerful growth.* 11 July 2011. www.socialenterpriselive.com/section/se100/management/20110711/vibrant-sector-defies-downturn-powerful-growth

59 Community-Wealth. *Overview: Community Stock Ownership Plans (ESOPS).* http://community-wealth.org/strategies/panel/esops/index.html

60 Brancatelli, J. (2012) *Why air travel has become so expensive, annoying, and cramped.* The Business Journals. 24 October 2012.
www.bizjournals.com/bizjournals/blog/seat2B/2012/10/
government-offers-air-travel-report.html?page=all

61 City and County of San Francisco, Office of the Mayor (2011)
Mayor Lee signs urban agriculture legislation for greater local food production in SF. 20 April 2011. www.sfmayor.org/index.
aspx?page=353/

62 Co-operative News (2012) *Power of co-operation: members outnumber shareholders by three to one.* 11 January 2012. www.thenews.coop/
article/power-co-operation-members-outnumber-shareholders-
three-one/

Chapter 2

1   Kingsnorth, P. (2008) *Real England: the battle against the bland.*
Portobello Books.

2   An argument explored in Trainer, T. (2007) *Renewable Energy Cannot Sustain a Consumer Society.* Springer.

3   From a speech he gave, the video and transcript of which can be found in a post called *Former German President waxes lyrical about Transition* at http://transitionculture.org/2013/05/07/
former-german-president-waxes-lyrical-about-transition/

4   From research conducted by Helen Beetham into the impact of Transition Streets in Totnes, *Social Impacts of Transition Together (SITT): investigating the social impacts, benefits and sustainability of the Transition Together / Transition Streets initiative in Totnes.* Available at
www.transitiontogether.org.uk/wp-content/uploads/2012/07/
SocialimpactsofTransitionStreets-finalreport.pdf

5   Watts, N. (2012) *Gasketeers win the fight for eco lights. Ledbury Reporter.* 21 February 2012.
http://www.ledburyreporter.co.uk/news/9541640.print/

6   The Local Resilience Action Plan can be downloaded from
www.scribd.com/doc/71442230/Sustaining-Dunbar-2025-
Local-Resilience-Action-Plan

7   Bristol Pound (2012) *The Queen to be presented with unique set of Bristol Pounds*. 22 November 2012. www.bristolpound.org/news?id=12

8   Morris, S. (2012) *Mayor to take salary in Bristol Pounds*. *The Guardian*. 20 November 2012. www.guardian.co.uk/uk/2012/nov/20/mayor-salary-bristol-pounds

9   Cohn, R. (2013) *Charting a new course for the U.S. and the environment*. Yale Environment 360.
http://e360.yale.edu/feature/interview_gus_speth_charting_new_course_for_us_and_environment/2612/

10   As discussed at http://transitionculture.org/2012/09/10/transition-appears-in-a-level-global-citizenship-exam-questions/

11   Hughes, T. (2004) *The Dreamfighter and Other Creation Tales*. Faber and Faber.

Chapter 3

1   All available at www.transitionnetwork.org

2   Finley, R. (2013) *Ron Finley: a guerilla gardener in South Central LA*. A TED Talk. http://www.ted.com/talks/ron_finley_a_guerilla_gardener_in_south_central_la.html

3   One that really stands out is Anne Evans and Peter Segger's Blaencamel Farm in North Wales. The King and Queen of compost-making.

4   The ingredient 'Community Brainstorming Tools' can be found at http://www.transitionnetwork.org/tools/connecting/community-brainstorming-tools

5   A concept explored in depth at Eisenstein, C. (2011) *Money, Gift and Community in an Age of Transition*. Evolver Editions. Available to read online free at www.sacred-economics.com/read-online/

6   Smith, C. (2012) *Transition Town Fujino goes for local energy independence*. OurWorld 2.0. 26 October 2012. http://ourworld.unu.edu/en/transition-town-fujino-goes-for-local-energy-independence/

Chapter 4

1 Nelson, J. (2013) *Co-op breweries: craft beer in the new economy.* PostGrowth.org. 22 February 2013. http://postgrowth.org/co-op-breweries-craft-beer-in-the-new-economy/

2 Leach, K. (2013) *Why mainstream Community Economic Development? Because it works.* REconomy.org. 7 March 2013. http://www.reconomy.org/why-mainstream-community-economic-development-because-it-works/

3 Thevard, B., Cochet, Y. (2013) *Europe facing peak oil.* The Greens/EFA Group in the European Parliament. Available from www.peakoil-europaction.eu/blocs/page.html

4 www.reconomy.org

5 You can see a film I made about the 2013 Totnes Local Entrepreneurs' Forum at www.transitionculture.org/2013/04/02/a-taste-of-the-future-in-the-community-of-dragons/

6 Beckett, E. N. (2013) *Transition Town Brixton launches pioneering analysis to reveal the benefits of a local economy.* Transition Town Brixton. 28 February 2013. www.transitiontownbrixton.org/2013/02/transition-town-brixton-launches-pioneering-analysis-to-uncover-the-benefits-of-localising-lambeths-economy/

A few closing thoughts

1 Castells, M. (2012) *Networks of Outrage and Hope: social movements in the internet age.* Polity Press.

Resources*

Here are some useful resources to get you started with exploring some of the themes and ideas covered in this book:

Food

Lawrence, F. (2008) *Eat Your Heart Out: why the food business is bad for the planet and your health* (Penguin)

Local United has created *Setting up a Local Food Hub: a guide for schools*: http://tinyurl.com/cnwwszz

Pinkerton, T. & Hopkins, R. (2009) *Local Food: how to make it happen in your community* (Transition Books / Green Books). Available as an e-book only.

Soil Association has produced *A share in the harvest: an action manual for community supported agriculture*, which can be downloaded at http://tinyurl.com/bu6a97q, and the very useful *Cultivating co-operatives: organisational structures for local food enterprises*: http://tinyurl.com/bt8u984

TransitionCulture.org has a digest of food-related activities that Transition groups have engaged in, with videos and lots of links: www.transitionculture.org/2012/06/29/transition-essentials-no-1-food

Energy

Bird, C. (2010) *Local Sustainable Homes: how to make them happen in your community* (Transition Books / Green Books)

----

* A set of these Resources with live hyperlinks can be downloaded from www.greenbooks.co.uk/The-Power-Of-Just-Doing-Stuff.html

Clark, D. & Chadwick, M., *The Rough Guide to Community Energy* is an excellent concise overview of your options and possibilities: www.roughguide.to/communityenergy

Local United has produced a series of guides to setting up community renewable projects, including:
Community-led hydro initiatives: inspiring overview of hydro installations, funding and project profit management: www.localunited.net/sites/default/files/Local_United_Hydro_Diffusion_Pack_Jan2011c.pdf
Community-led wind power: how to plan, build and own a medium or large wind turbine in your community's backyard: www.localunited.net/sites/default/files/Local_United_Wind_Diffusion_Pack_Jan2011c.pdf

Pahl, G. (2012) *Power from the People: how to organize, finance and launch local energy projects* (Chelsea Green Publishing)

The Scottish Government has published an excellent *Community Renewable Energy Toolkit*: www.scotland.gov.uk/Resource/Doc/917/0115761.pdf

Shepherd, A., Allen, P. & Harper, P. (2012) *The Home Energy Handbook: a guide to saving and generating energy in your home and community* (Centre for Alternative Technology Publications)

Local currencies

Bristol Pound have an excellent 'What is it?' section at http://bristolpound.org/what

The Cheimgauer is a fascinating regional currency model from southern Germany. Here is an article about it: www.guardian.co.uk/money/2011/sep/23/local-currencies-german-chiemgauer

Dudok Van Heel, O. (2009) *The Lewes Pound: a Transition Network 'how to' guide*: www.transitionculture.org/wp-content/uploads/Lewes-Pound-How-To-Guide.pdf

Hallsmith, G. and Lietaer, B.'s (2011) book *Creating Wealth: growing local economies with local currencies* (New Society Publishers) is also a good overview.

North, P. (2010) *Local Money: how to make it happen in your community* (Transition Books / Green Books)

Shuman, M. (2012) *Local Dollars, Local Sense: how to shift your money from Wall Street to Main Street and achieve real prosperity* (Chelsea Green Publishing)

Working with your local council

Rowell, A. (2010) *Communities, Councils and a Low-Carbon Future: what we can do if governments won't* (Transition Books / Green Books)

Some key books for illuminating our predicament, and why business-as-usual is over

Hamilton, C. (2010) *Requiem for a Species: why we resist the truth about climate change* (Earthscan)

Heinberg, R. (2011) *The End of Growth: adapting to our new economic reality* (Clairview Publications)

Heinberg, R. & Lerch, D. (2010) *The Post Carbon Reader: managing the 21st century's sustainability crises* (Post Carbon Institute / Watershed Media)

Homer-Dixon, T. (2007) *The Upside of Down: catastrophe, creativity and the renewal of civilisation* (Souvenir Press)

Johnson, V., Simms, A., Skrebowski, C. & Greenham, T. (2012) *The economics of oil dependence: a glass ceiling to recovery. Why the oil industry today is like banking was in 2006* (New Economics Foundation)

Kasser, T. (2002) *The High Price of Materialism* (MIT Press)

Kingsnorth, P. (2008) *Real England: the battle against the bland* (Portobello Books)

Klein, N. (2008) *The Shock Doctrine: the rise of disaster capitalism* (Penguin)

Lewis, M. & Conaty, P. (2012) *The Resilience Imperative: cooperative transitions to a steady-state economy* (New Society Publishers)

Simms, A. (2007) *Tescopoly: how one shop came out on top and why it matters* (Constable)

Some suggested DVDs

Here are the top 10 films (in descending order) as chosen by Transition initiatives, and where to get them:

In Transition 1.0 (available to watch at www.vimeo.com/8029815) and *In Transition 2.0* (can be ordered from www.intransitionmovie.com)

A Farm for the Future (can be watched on YouTube)

The Power of Community (available from www.powerofcommunity.org)

Koyaanisqatsi (can be watched on YouTube)

The Economics of Happiness (available from www.theeconomicsofhappiness.org)

The Age of Stupid (available from www.dogwoof.com/films/the-age-of-stupid)

Voices of the Transition (available from www.voicesoftransition.org)

Dirt, the Movie (available from www.thedirtmovie.org)

There's No Tomorrow (can be watched on YouTube)

The End of Suburbia (available from www.endofsuburbia.com)

Other places where you can find inspiring stories

Flintoff, J. P. (2012) *How to Change the World* (The School of Life)

Holmgren, D. (2003) *Permaculture: principles and pathways beyond sustainability* (Holmgren Design Services)

Permaculture magazine (www.permaculture.co.uk) and *Permaculture Activist* magazine (www.permacultureactivist.net)

Spratt, S., Simms, A., Neitzert, E. & Ryan-Collins, J. (2009) *The Great Transition: a tale of how it turned out right* (New Economics Foundation)

Places where you could acquire some new skills

The Centre for Alternative Technology, Machynlleth, Wales, which offers an amazing range of courses and trainings: www.cat.org.uk

The Hollies Centre for Practical Sustainability, West Cork, Ireland, of which the author was one of the founders: www.thehollies.ie

One Year in Transition, a new programme from Transition Network: www.transitionnetwork.org/support/education/one-year-transition

Permaculture Association (UK) has a great list of courses: www.permaculture.org.uk

Schools in Transition: www.transitionnetwork.org/support/education/schools-transition

The Village, an eco-village in Cloughjordan, Ireland: www.thevillage.ie

Index

Also published by Green Books

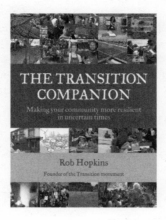

The Transition Companion
Making your community more resilient
in uncertain times
by Rob Hopkins

The Transition Companion describes one of the most fascinating experiments now underway in the world. It shows how communities are working for a future where local enterprises are valued and nurtured; where lower energy use is seen as a benefit; and where cooperation, creativity and the building of resilience are the cornerstones of a new economy.

About Green Books

Join our mailing list:
Find out about forthcoming titles, new editions, special offers,
reviews, author appearances, events, interviews, podcasts, etc.
www.greenbooks.co.uk/subscribe

How to order:
Get details of stockists and online bookstores. (Remember that you
can also order direct from our website.) If you are a bookstore, find
out about our distributors or contact us to discuss your particular
requirements.
www.greenbooks.co.uk/order

Send us a book proposal:
If you want to write – even if you have just the kernel of an idea
at present – we'd love to hear from you. We pride ourselves on
supporting our authors and making the process of book-writing
as satisfying and as easy as possible.
www.greenbooks.co.uk/for-authors